The Team Coach

Vital New Skills for Supervisors & Managers in a Team Environment

Donna Deeprose

amacom

American Management Association

New York • Atlanta • Boston • Chicago • Kansas City • San Francisco • Washington, D.C.
Brussels • Mexico City • Tokyo • Toronto

This publication is designed to provide accurate and authoritative information in regard to the subject matter covered. It is sold with the understanding that the publisher is not engaged in rendering legal, accounting, or other professional service. If legal advice or other expert assistance is required, the services of a competent professional person should be sought.

Library of Congress Cataloging-in-Publication Data

Deeprose, Donna.
    The team coach: vital new skills for supervisors & managers in
  a team environment / Donna Deeprose.
      p. cm.
  Includes bibliographical references and index.
  ISBN 0-8144-7859-X
  1. Supervision of employees.   2. Work groups.   I. Title.
HF5549.12.L44   1995
658.3'02 — dc20   95-638
                                              CIP

Printing number

10 9 8 7 6

Contents

Acknowledgments

I owe the existence of this book to a group of dedicated team champions in a number of companies. They were generous in sharing their time, their experiences, and their expertise when I asked them to tell me all about coaching self-directed work teams. My first interviewees, Brenda Dietrich of Honeywell and Fred Eintracht of Texas Instruments, got me started on a journey of many months to learn from practitioners who were making a difference in their organizations.

Fred connected me to a group of his colleagues at Texas Instruments: Bill Crockett, Tom Howes, Pete Keller, and Karen Page, all of whom took the time to answer my questions thoughtfully and in depth. So did all the wonderful people I talked to in other companies: Wanda Vinson, Wilma Weed, and Krissan Zoby at Bell Atlantic; Jerry Labadini, Bill Harding, and Joe Reece of General Electric; Patty Barten, Michelle Thomas, Joan Clarke, and Diane Lewis, who showed me their operation at Motorola; Chuck Stridde and Tim Smith of Northern Telecom; and Chris Ward, Kevin Roberts, Dave Litwin, and Ralph Galarneau, who welcomed me when I visited their Titeflex plant. I want to thank all of them for all they taught me. To Tom Howes of Texas Instruments and Tim Smith of Northern Telecom I owe an additional thanks for sharing the documents included in this book.

Richard Plumley of Plumley Companies didn't know he was destined to be quoted here when I interviewed him on a different topic. When I told him what the book was about, he agreed to be included.

I also want to thank my friends and colleagues who

provided support and expertise: Roz Gold, who pushed me past my procrastination by calling me many mornings and *directing* me to write; Eleanor Hamill, who gave me a lesson on budgeting; and Karen Massoni, Jane Cooper, and Katherine Marsala, who filled in gaps in my research.

Lastly, because it's customary to leave spouses until the last, thanks to you, Ralph, for editing my work brilliantly when I got bogged down, and for those endless cups of cinnamon coffee that kept me going as I worked on this manuscript night after night.

Introduction: Changing Times, Changing Roles

In the 1950s and 1960s it seemed as if American business had reached an apogee in production know-how. Nowhere else, never before had so many industries spawned so many products destined for the waiting arms of a consuming public with such an insatiable appetite. Everything from hula hoops to jet planes poured out of factories that would have made Frederick Taylor, the father of scientific management, swell with pride. Following his guidelines,[1] on production lines — and in offices, too — millions of workers all performed narrowly defined tasks over and over, under the watchful eyes of management. Managers did the thinking and directing that linked all the individual tasks into a completed product.

It worked. Businesses, managers, and workers all prospered.

Then, slowly at first but soon picking up momentum, competition from abroad began to make inroads into the marketplace, onto the highways, and right into the kitchens and living rooms of America. By the mid-1970s, that competition had ceased to be a mere irritant and had become a mortal threat. And by the 1980s, Western companies — from entrepreneurial start-ups to industry giants — had become painfully aware that the enemy was not Japan or Korea but

---

1. Frederick W. Taylor, *The Principles of Scientific Management* (New York: Wiley, 1911).

1

their own cavalier attitude toward customer wants and needs, quality, and outdated work processes.

A Stage Set for Change

As businesses examined their own operations, they discovered needs, omissions, and some tragically underused resources:

- The need to reduce costs while improving quality and service
- The need to cut through inflated layers of management that had swelled to the point of blocking communication and slowing production
- The need to listen to customers, treat them with respect, give them the quality they expect and deserve, and respond instantly to their problems
- The need to simplify and improve work processes, paring them down to just those tasks necessary to meet customer requirements
- The need to utilize more fully the experience and knowledge of the people closest to production, the workers who make the product or deliver the service
- The need to improve production despite personnel reductions through downsizings

Rising to the Challenge: Self-Directed Work Teams

Meeting all these needs requires nothing less than a revolution in the workplace, a new way of organizing work and people that transcends the rigid boundaries that have compartmentalized workers, stifled innovation at the grass-roots level, and separated the people producing the product or service from the people consuming it.

The leaders of the revolution are organizations that

are converting to self-directed work teams, which address many of these needs by putting decision-making and problem-solving authority in the hands of the people closest to the product or service and the customer. A self-directed work team (SDWT) is:

> A small group of employees who share responsibilities for a block of work, usually the production of a specific product or group of related products or the delivery of a particular service or group of services. The team has the responsibility and the authority to plan, schedule, and assign work and to make and implement decisions related to production and personnel.

In companies where SDWTs have taken hold, they have redrawn the face of the organization and revitalized operations, leading to marked improvements in productivity, quality, and customer satisfaction. General Electric's Plant III in Lynn, Massachusetts, for example, which makes aircraft engines, is a world apart from the management-heavy operation of the early 1980s, from which it evolved. Instead of reporting to a foreman, who reported to a unit manager, who reported to a subsection manager, who reported to the plant manager, operators now work in cells, or teams, that report directly to the plant manager.

The teams manage their own work, supported by one cell leader for each shift for all four teams. They've learned maintenance, statistical process control, and people-management skills. And instead of operating single machines, workers are skilled in running all the machines in the plant. Some are capable of building an entire jet engine on their own.

The team-based plant has experienced cost savings of 30 percent, quality improvement of 33 percent, reduction in cycle time from ten weeks to two, and reduction in manufacturing losses from 4 percent to 2 1/2 percent. When GE recently moved production of a part there from its most productive plant, in Wilmington, North Carolina, the teams at Plant III immediately cut Wilmington's production time by a third.[2]

Facing New Challenges: Supervisors in a New Role

Teams capable of managing themselves don't emerge over-night, fully developed, from the ether. They need training, encouraging, and guiding, and often they need someone to run interference for them as they try out their newly found power.

These responsibilities usually land directly on supervisors, who are often reeling from rounds of downsizing that have decimated the ranks of management and left them uncertain survivors afloat in untested lifeboats. They are armed with a set of outdated directing and controlling skills and often lack mentors or role models, since top-level managers have no more experience with team-based structures than do supervisors.

As this book will show, many supervisors rise to the challenge and throw themselves wholeheartedly into the grand new adventure of supporting the revitalization of their operations. Others, however, lose their bearings, as well as their confidence in their ability to contribute to the organization. Instead of receiving support and guidance, they are given enough rope to hang themselves — and sometimes they do.

Even in companies that successfully launch SDWTs, the fallout rate among supervisors is about 25 percent.[3] These supervisors fail to develop the new skills they need and are unable to carry out their new responsibilities. So they leave, or the organization forces them out. Among those who stay, another sizable group muddles along at less than full poten-

2. Personal correspondence from Jerry Labadini, plant manager of GE Plant III, Lynn, Mass., October 31, 1994.
3. Jana Schilder, "Work Teams Boost Productivity," *Personnel Journal*, February 1992, pp. 67–71.

tial until they escape resentfully into some other job in the organization.

What a waste of organizational, technical, and administrative know-how! These are people who have both a thorough knowledge of production and a grasp of management expectations. They have an important role to play in helping teams perform their new duties.

Reversing the Brain Drain

The purpose of this book is to help organizations prevent that brain drain, to give supervisors and others charged with supporting teams the resources they need to get up to speed quickly in the new situation, and to provide teams with the support they require to succeed.

It focuses on the role of the "team coach," a generic term for the people charged with transferring management responsibilities to teams; providing teams with training, technical, and counseling resources; facilitating team development and mediating conflicts; bolstering teams when they stumble; and cheerleading for them from the time they take their first tentative steps until they emerge as mature, truly self-directed teams.

These people may go by any of a number of titles: adviser, facilitator, team developer, cell leader, team manager, business unit manager. In some organizations, the job description changes, but the title does not; it remains supervisor. Whatever their titles, the practitioners interviewed for this book all related to the word "coach," agreeing that it describes what they do.

This book describes what SDWTs do for themselves that supervisors used to do, what help they still need, and what skills team coaches require to provide that help. It breaks down the coach's role into functions and tasks and provides guidelines for performing them.

The skills and practices described in this book are based, not on theory, but on what works in organizations — like GE's Plant III in Lynn — that are outperforming traditional operations. The information comes from interviews with a score of coaches, managers, and team champions ranging from internal organization development consultants to a union steward. All quotes throughout the book come from these personal interviews, conducted from spring 1994 through early 1995.

Who This Book Is For . . .

This is a book for supervisors and former supervisors in organizations that have created or are experimenting with SDWTs. It is also for their managers, who need to coach the coaches and who, increasingly, will find themselves dealing directly with worker teams. In addition, it's for trainers who are being called upon to teach the new skills and for organization development professionals supporting the sweeping change in structure and relationships.

It's not necessary to work in a restructured company to find value in this book. There is plenty here for supervisors and managers in traditional organizations who recognize that they can increase their effectiveness in any setting by behaving more like coaches and less like cops.

Part I

The Changing Face
of the Workplace

Self-directed work teams? Once, just the suggestion of such a thing would have been scoffed at as "turning the asylum over to the inmates." Now SDWTs are being hailed as a solution to falling productivity, rising costs, and stagnating responsiveness to customer needs. The first part of this book illustrates how teams revolutionize the workplace, reversing the traditional manager/worker relationship, and describes the impact of teams in both business and human terms.

1

The Team Revolution

One fateful Friday in 1989, without warning, Titeflex Corporation of Springfield, Massachusetts, which produces flexible hose for the automotive and aerospace industries, eliminated the jobs of all twenty-five of its supervisors in its Hendee Street plant. Of the group, the company retained only a handful, reassigning about five to technical or administrative positions and naming three to the newly created position of team manager. Team managers were expected to coach and support teams of workers, rather than perform traditional supervisory functions.

The painful task of informing the supervisors fell to Operations Manager Kevin Roberts. He claims to have locked himself in his office the following Monday and stayed in there for two weeks.

During those two weeks he sent "spies" to see what was happening in the factory, where the all-union workforce had been plunged into self-management. The first day, his informant told him, everybody was just milling around. The second day, he learned that one worker had tired of waiting for someone to tell him what to do and started working on a job. Gradually, the other workers followed his lead. Not only did they go back to their old production jobs, but they picked up the management and administrative tasks needed to keep production rolling. At Titeflex, self-directed work teams (SDWTs) were born that Monday.

Titeflex's aerospace teams are small groups of employees, each responsible for the production of a defined product group (except for one team that is dedicated to satisfying the needs of Titeflex's biggest customer, General Electric).

They schedule their own time and assign jobs, manage their own budgets and buy their own supplies, hire their own people and participate in hiring technical support people, and communicate directly with customers.

Titeflex is one of an increasing number of organizations — ranging from manufacturing companies to health care providers — that have shifted traditional supervisory responsibilities to teams of workers. Few companies, however, have made the switch quite so abruptly. At Bell Atlantic, for example, where workers in several service offices have been reorganized into teams, the teams are assuming sensitive tasks like hiring and disciplining team members in stages, gradually increasing their autonomy.

Self-directed work teams are one of a number of types of teams — others are cross-functional teams, product improvement teams, and process improvement teams — that are changing the look of companies everywhere. At Motorola's Cellular Products Division in Arlington Heights, Illinois, several kinds of teams overlap. Any individual who sees an opportunity to make an improvement and who can make a strong case for an innovative idea has the right to request other workers to join a team. By this method, employees have formed teams that have won recognition and rewards for their product, process, or quality improvement.

But these are temporary teams. What distinguishes SDWTs is that they are permanent, full-time work assignments. At Motorola, each employee is part of a work team that makes a product or product component, where all team members share responsibility for running their operation like a small business.

Behind the Revolution, an Evolution

No company waves a magic wand and turns individual workers into teams skilled at running a business overnight — or over one weekend. Not even Titeflex. There, self-directed teams may have been "born" that Monday when the workers found themselves with no bosses. But the gestation period had begun a few years earlier, when the company first organized workers into manufacturing cells with the goal of speeding up cycle time and getting products more quickly into customers' hands. Those early cells operated in an environment where, according to Christopher J. Ward, general manager of Bulk Hose/Automotive, "managers wore six-guns and hid behind posts." Their message to workers was, "Don't breathe unless I tell you."

Things began to change in 1988 under a new president who became convinced that, by removing the "manager as cop" and involving workers in decision making, he could radically speed up the company's slow response to customer orders and reverse Titeflex's slide into nonprofitability.

To change the culture at Titeflex, he needed the cooperation of the union as well as management. Chief Steward Ralph R. Galarneau recalls, "The president called me and said he wanted to change the culture. I thought, 'Right. He really wants to bust the union.'" But the president's promise that workers would participate in the design of new processes at Titeflex was compelling and began to break down Galarneau's skepticism. Says Galarneau, "I told him, 'Just don't lie to me. I want the good news and the bad.'"

From small changes, like the elimination of preferred parking and time clocks, to big ones like joint management/worker training in running a business, the evidence grew that Titeflex's top management really was playing a different tune. "Previously, the message to workers had been: Come to work, leave your brains outside, and do what you are told," explains Roberts, echoing a refrain that is part of the lore among the committed at Titeflex. "Now the message was: Please bring your brains with you, and learn how to run a business."

Galarneau was confident enough to support the process even though one worker warned him, only half in jest, that if it didn't work out, the police would find him in a swamp somewhere. "We were evolving, leading up to that Friday," he remembers. Somewhat to his surprise, the first to buy in to the new structure were long-term employees, who acted as role models to the others.

Real Change or "Program of the Month"?

For many of the managers, who had been brought up on Frederick Taylor's principles of scientific management, the change was threatening, on the one hand, and lacking in credibility, on the other. After all, they'd been through what Roberts calls "the program-of-the-month club" before. Inside management ranks there was some deep-rooted resistance to empowering work teams. Sometimes this opposition manifested itself in passive-aggressive behavior. In the early days of change as roles were evolving, one supervisor announced to his employees, "Now we're all self-directed. Just take what jobs you want." Washing his hands of all responsibility, he watched from the sidelines as workers vied unproductively for the plum assignments.

Another supervisor had an employee who came to work in a ripped T-shirt, with flowing hair and with a boom box on his shoulder. To communicate his displeasure when the company took away preferred parking, the supervisor began showing up bedecked in the same way.

For all their planning and training, the empowerment champions at Titeflex realized that only a drastic, revolutionary step would jolt their vision into reality. To send a signal to both the workforce and management that Titeflex was serious, Friday, they say, had to happen. The firings transformed Titeflex from a company trying to evolve into empowerment into one where the workers had to manage their own day-to-day activities because there simply wasn't anyone else around to do it for them.

Redefining Management's Role

The hourly workers weren't the only ones who needed to redefine their roles. The three people who came to work that Monday as new team managers, and the few who have stepped into the role since then, had to find their way in a new environment where most of their old skills were not only obsolete but in direct contradiction to the way the company was determined to operate.

But if the teams of workers were self-managing, what was left for a team manager to do?

Plenty, apparently, starting with providing leadership, resources, and training.

"The job is to work for the people, and also to provide leadership and vision," says Roberts. That involves "helping workers identify what the goals are, implanting a vision of where we want to go."

"Get the workers what they need to do the job," adds Team Manager Dave Litwin, a staunch supporter and self-proclaimed cheerleader for his thirteen teams. "I put my six-shooters back on when one of my people says, 'I went to see so-and-so and she said she didn't have time to talk to me.'"

"There's a lot of training that's ongoing, every day. It's the Daves [Litwin] that do that," adds Galarneau, who speaks from a union worker's point of view.

At Titeflex, everyone agrees that the team manager's role is much more demanding than in the old days when supervisors had scripted answers to problems.

If managing self-directed teams is so much more difficult than managing individual workers, why use them? What's the appeal of this new way of operating? And will it last, or is it another trendy panacea?

Wave of the Future or Wave of the Hand?

On a small scale, SDWTs have been around a long time. Credit for introducing modern autonomous teams usually goes to Yorkshire coal miners, who as early as the 1940s were working in small groups to direct their own activity.[1] Although the system didn't exactly spread like wildfire, Proc-

1. Eric L. Trist and W. Bamforth, "Some Social and Psychological Consequences of the Longwall Method of Coal Getting," *Human Relations* 4, no. 1 (1951): 3–38.

ter & Gamble in the United States introduced autonomous teams into several plants in the 1960s and kept very quiet about them; the team-based plants were so productive that the company considered them a competitive secret.

Even when word leaked out about the higher productivity, lower turnover, and better quality in P&G's plants, other companies didn't rush to jump on the bandwagon. In the 1970s and early 1980s, as American industry, stigmatized by falling productivity, high costs, and lack of responsiveness to customers, faltered in both global and domestic markets, the most commonly offered solution to the problem was to throw more — not less — management at it. After all, solving problems was management's job. That was something that both managers and many union workers agreed on.

Many companies that did try teams in the 1980s abandoned them prematurely. Successful implementation is hard, and often companies found the changeover frustratingly slow, with few tangible benefits at first. "You've got to ride through a period of sitting in meetings that seems to last forever," admits Roberts of Titeflex. "People rise to levels at their own pace. You can't force them."

But the problems of the late 1980s and early 1990s did not respond to traditional solutions, and companies switched to cutting, not adding, management, while they tested new quality initiatives and sought to improve their responsiveness to customer needs. As they strove to shore up crumbling customer bases, some companies slipped into self-directed team structures by the side door. First, they discovered their new process improvement techniques worked only when the people performing the tasks got involved in areas that had previously been the domain of management or professional support. When the workers created the floor plans, for example, work flowed faster.

Texas Instruments' Defense Systems Group started its first experiments with what it calls empowered business teams around 1987. "In our manufacturing areas we were starting to look at work more as a process than as a series of tasks," recalls Fred Eintracht, manager of High Performing Organization Development, who was a driving force behind those teams. "We started to notice that if we gave the people doing the work more responsibility to develop methodology the results were significantly better." And when people took responsibility for making commitments to customers regarding costs and schedules, they also took more ownership for meeting those commitments.

The results were so good that Eintracht and a handful of managers began to explore SDWTs more directly, nurturing a few teams in pockets throughout the Defense Systems Group. By 1991 upper management had taken notice of their success, and the use of teams was formalized within the unit. Just a year later, in 1992, the team-based Defense Systems Group won the Malcolm Baldrige National Quality Award.

Are companies like Texas Instruments, Titeflex, and General Electric riding the wave of the future as they transform at least parts of their businesses into team-based operations? Team champions in these organizations are convinced that self-directed work teams have a big role to play in their futures. Although SDWTs are neither a panacea nor a quick fix, they are having a major impact in companies that have the conviction and the diligence to stick out the turmoil that inevitably accompanies the implementation of major organizational change.

2

The Impact of Teams

Why have teams suddenly caught on in so many companies? More than anything, perhaps, it's the life-or-death situations many organizations confront. Like Titeflex, Texas Instruments Defense Systems Group turned to teams when it was standing on the brink of major change, confronting the loss of its markets as defense spending dried up. Says Peter Keller, former cost center manager at Texas Instruments and now a mentor for team facilitators, "A lot of things were going on that made us realize if we didn't do something different, we wouldn't have a business."

What a difference teams have made for many companies in need of a major business turnaround. In the 1980s Titeflex was so unprofitable that many analysts predicted its demise; by the mid-1990s it was making a tidy profit. Whereas in the past it turned over its inventory just twice a year, turnover improved to six times, with most work being done lot for lot, to meet individual orders. As recently as 1990, when Titeflex workers visited General Electric's Lynn, Massachusetts, aircraft engine facilities, they remarked on how few hoses had come from Titeflex and how many from competitors. A GE employee explained why, exclaiming, "We're sick and tired of waiting because you can't deliver on time." But just a few years later, GE Lynn representatives visited Titeflex to study its team system and used the Titeflex model to revitalize their own Plant III.

With teams of self-directed workers, GE's Plant III accomplished what it had failed to achieve with a fully automated, robotized Factory of the Future of the early 1980s, reducing cycle time to a fraction of what it had been. In January 1994, for example, Plant III took over production of a part from one of GE's most productive plants. Plant III's production goal was forty-three hours per part. After a slow start (104 hours the first week), Plant III met its goal within ten months, reports Cell Leader Bill Harding, outpacing the previous maker, whose best time was fifty-six hours. Assigned to manufacture a part that had previously been made at the company's Wilmington factory, Plant III beat the Wilmington time in its first week and has bested Wilmington's annual average cost by 28 percent.

But it is not just numbers that attest to the triumph of team-based operations. Patty Barten, vice president of Motorola's Cellular Products Division, which began converting its production lines to autonomous teams in 1987, measures success primarily by the attitudes of employees. Teams are better, she asserts, "because the people themselves say so. They want to stay here, better themselves, know more about the business." And, yes, she also has hard facts. "Twice a year we check the hard metrics," she says. "We've found a two-to-one improvement in efficiency, space, volume of output per employee, and number of managers per person."

Within two years of instituting a team approach, Bell Atlantic's sales and service offices had felt the benefit of the change. Wilma Weed, assistant manager and team developer in the Silver Springs, Maryland, Interexchange Carrier Service Center, says the team system has been a win/win situation for everybody. "Service reps are happier. They make wonderful decisions. Customers are happier."

Deciding what indices to track to measure their success, the Bell Atlantic teams chose variables that are important for keeping the customers happy. "It's difficult to keep up with all the new things we offer and to keep track of everything in the mechanized system, so errors can occur that cause delays in billing," Weed explains. "When an order falls to error, we have to go in and correct it. The new tracking and measuring system identifies what caused the error, and the team makes sure it is fixed for the next time, so it doesn't happen again."

Figure 2–1. MCB organization chart.

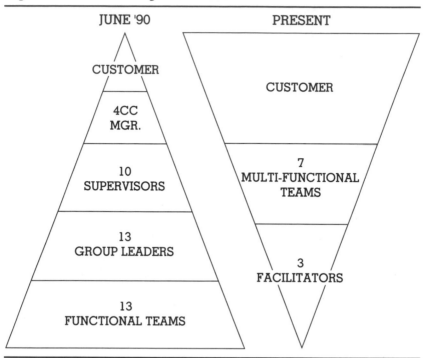

Source: Tom Howes, Teaming Process Manager, Lewisville Center for Excellence, Defense Systems and Electronics Group, Texas Instruments. Used with permission.

The New Organization

Teams have the potential to improve organizational results dramatically. The price they extract is a complete overhaul in organizational structure and organizational thinking. Figure 2–1 illustrates the upheaval in the structure at a Texas Instruments Microwave Circuit Board shop, where sixty-nine nonexempt employees produce 120 systems per month. Even the facilitators, who serve many of the same coaching functions as Titeflex's team managers and Bell Atlantic's team developers, are nonexempt employees. In 1990, 187 people, including a salaried management staff of 14, worked in the shop, turning out two hundred systems per month; three layers of management separated the workers from the customers. The new system, in contrast, puts the team members in direct customer contact, supported by facilitators trained in business operations, problem solving, team support, coaching, conflict management, and a variety of other technical, social, and administrative skills. Propping up the new pyramid is a small leadership team that supports and mentors the facilitators.

If there is a victim in this change, it appears to be the old-style supervisor, whose job is transformed beyond recognition or even disappears. Although few organizations do away with supervisors as dramatically as did Titeflex, the need for them diminishes as teams take over responsibilities that were once supervisors' private domains. Texas Instruments' Fabrication Shop in Sherman, Texas, no longer even has facilitators. "The teams matured beyond them," states Bill Crockett, Responsibility Center manager.

But the route to full team maturity is pitted with hazards that call for the coaching and facilitation skills of former supervisors and managers who champion change. Supporting team development is a bigger role than many organizations recognize at the outset. When Bell Atlantic's Consumer Sales unit in Beltsville, Maryland, first organized into teams, Assistant Manager Wanda Vinson became team developer for three teams. But coaching three teams, each with its own responsibilities and personality, proved unrealistic. Now she works with just one.

Self-directed work teams don't get that way by declaration. They need nurturing, coaching, encouragement, and the support of someone to pave their paths to customers, suppliers, and upper management. Those responsibilities fall to the team coach.

Part II

Making the Transition From Supervisor to Coach

Just how big a change is it, this adjustment from traditional supervisor to team coach? The next chapters examine what teams do for themselves that supervisors used to do, what teams still need, and what coaches do to meet those needs. Then, we look at the qualities—outlook and skills—that a coach needs to succeed.

3

Letting Go

In making the transition from traditional assistant manager to team developer in Bell Atlantic's Consumer Sales unit, the biggest challenge, says Wanda Vinson, is letting go of control: "Before, I had total responsibility for making things happen. If not, I had to give up an account. In the new environment, that responsibility is shared."

Wilma Weed, in Bell Atlantic's Interexchange Carrier Service Center, echoes the thought. The big change, she says, has been from controlling to supporting. "'Give me the work and I'll get it done for you' was my credo," she recalls. "I looked at the amount of work and the number of people and figured out whom I should give what tasks to. You learn to make decisions very quickly in that environment."

Now Weed is learning to restrain that urge to make decisions and to leave them to the teams. It's a lesson that gets constant reinforcement. Weed tells of a situation in which a team member came to her and said, "Wilma, I want to change my hours and come in at 8:15 instead of 7:30."

"Fine, no problem," Weed replied. "Just go to the team and make sure they know."

But that wasn't good enough. Soon afterward, the team leader (a rotating position) took her to task. "Wilma, we'd appreciate it if when you're asked those questions you wouldn't make those decisions so quickly. That was a decision for the team to make," the team leader reminded her. "We know our needs for covering the work."

Now, Weed says, she tries to remember to let the teams make decisions in those areas where teams have taken over responsibilities that used to be hers.

Figure 3–1.   What teams do.

New Teams	Maturing Teams	Mature Teams
Schedule work and assign tasks	Manage budgets	Determine overtime
Manage vacation schedules	Contact customers	Conduct performance appraisals
Keep attendance	Communicate with vendors	Discipline team members
Solve problems	Participate in planning	
Monitor results	Participate in goal setting	
Schedule training	Participate in hiring	

Team Responsibilities

What are supervisors being asked to let go of? What do self-directed teams do for themselves that supervisors used to do?

The answer depends, of course, upon the maturity of the team. When organizations make the choice to develop autonomous teams, they usually charge the new teams with responsibilities that grow as the teams mature. Team responsibilities may vary somewhat from organization to organization; the list in Figure 3–1 combines input from several organizations where teams are in all stages of development.

Responsibilities of New Teams

New teams may be asked to:

• *Schedule work and assign tasks.* Most companies find that the teams have a better handle than supervisors did on what new tasks each member is capable of assuming. "In my old role," Weed recalls, "work came to me and I passed it out, without consideration of what was on each service representative's desk already. I passed it out equally." Now the teams assign the work at morning "huddle meetings," where they talk about who has what on the desk and what work just came in.

"We're asking teams to make business decisions," says Karen Page, a business unit manager in Texas Instruments' McKinney Board Shop in McKinney, Texas. Teams in the circuit board facility have to understand business needs in order to set the priorities that determine who does what and when among the various presoldering, soldering, and post-soldering activities that happen day to day.

At GE's Plant III in Lynn, team members decide what the production priorities are and what jobs they should be running. Because they make these decisions, team members know they are working on the right hardware and using resources correctly.

• *Manage vacation schedules.* This includes covering for anyone who is out. Teams in Bell Atlantic's Interexchange Carrier Service Center in Silver Springs know that policy allows three people to be out at one time. One day Weed noticed four were out and asked why; the team members explained that an employee had a personal emergency, an appointment she couldn't change. The team had arranged to cover her work.

• *Keep attendance.* Page of Texas Instruments says that she was relieved to hand over to the team the task of "monitoring doors, watching if people came to work on time, a non-value-added supervisor duty associated with a traditional control mentality. As teams become accountable, the need to monitor attendance disappears."

• *Solve problems.* At Northern Telecom's Nashville Repair and Distribution Center, two initial responsibilities for teams are mandatory—"issue resolution," which requires the teams to take a team approach, use problem-solving methods, research, and follow-up; and "identify/solve problems."[1]

---

1. From a Northern Telecom internal communication titled "NRDC Self-Directed Work Teams, Job/Responsibilities Examples, February 15, 1994." Used with permission.

Teams are expected to have a system for identifying problems and to identify and implement solutions.

Similarly, at GE's Plant III, workers are bypassing the cell leader to get to the heart of a problem. "In the past," says Cell Leader Bill Harding, "if the workers had a technical problem, they'd come to me and I'd get a technical expert, say a planner or a maintenance person. Now they do that."

• *Monitor results.* Another mandatory team responsibility at Northern Telecom is "inspect own work." Teams develop their own systems for tracking their own progress and results.

"Before," says Weed of Bell Atlantic, "I had to go back and check at midday: Did everyone get half the work done? At day-end: Is the work all done? I had to know what everyone was doing during the course of the day. Now I don't even know what comes in."

• *Schedule training.* This includes arranging to cover a team member who is out being trained. In many companies, teams go one step further. Because one goal of most teams is to have all members trained in one another's jobs, team members also take on significant responsibility for developing and conducting training for one another. And staff downsizing places additional training burdens on the teams themselves. Weed says that the teams in her office not only schedule training and find the trainer but also write and conduct a lot of their own training. "One of my service reps just trained three new people for three weeks on how to take and process a service order," she reports. "She developed a binder and job aids and made room arrangements."

Responsibilities of Maturing Teams

As teams become more experienced in self-management, they usually take on additional responsibilities. The supervisor's role changes from performing these tasks for the team to nurturing the teams through trial and error and helping members learn from both their successes and their failures. With some successes under their belts and additional training, work teams are ready to:

• *Manage their own budgets.* This includes purchasing supplies. At Titeflex, when teams need small tools, often a member simply goes to the nearest hardware store. At Texas Instruments' Fabrication Shop in Sherman, Texas, teams approve their own orders of expense items up to $100.

• *Contact customers.* Motorola's Cellular Products Division sends groups of workers to visit customers as far away as Japan. At Titeflex, team members have even made sales pitches. Workers at Titeflex like to tell a story about a toolmaker who rides a Harley Davidson motorcycle. His co-workers describe him as "a typical biker; he wears a beard and a tank top." Harleys, they say, always leaked because they used rigid piping that often developed leaks from the bikes' vibrations. Taking scrap from Titeflex, the toolmaker piped up his Harley with flexible hose. Voila—no leaks.

"Let's call Harley," the toolmaker suggested, "and see if we can sell to them."

Management pitched in by finding a contact and told the toolmaker, "You call." So he did, and he aroused enough interest to get the Harley people to call back. But they called Marketing, which was not yet well acquainted with the empowered work teams in the plant.

Marketing complained to the plant managers, "You've got factory people talking to customers."

"What customer?" the plant managers responded. "You don't sell to Harley."

When Marketing went out and made its presentation to the motorcycle manufacturer, the Harley people replied, "Okay, we want to place an order, but not what you showed us. We want what the toolmaker uses."

Having work teams visit customers has another advantage, says Roberts of Titeflex. Sometimes the visitors get chewed out (remember the Titeflex workers' visit to the GE plant). When that happens, they come back and do something about the problem pronto. In contrast, when supervisors deliver criticisms from customers, workers often feel that management is just trying to get them to work harder.

• *Communicate with vendors.* Barten at Motorola recalls an incident with a supplier that arose because of a quality concern. A member of a manufacturing team recognized the problem. "We said, 'Okay, get on the phone with the designer at the supplier and get it solved.'" When that call didn't achieve the desired result, the worker kept pursuing the issue until he got an appointment with the president of the supplier company and got the problem solved.

• *Participate in planning.* At Northern Telecom's Nashville Repair and Distribution Center, Business Unit Manager Tim Smith (who calls himself a "recovering supervisor") works with teams that are equal partners in the annual planning process. At planning sessions, one-third of the group is made up of production floor team members, one-third are support team members (such as representatives of engineering, accounting, and production control), and one-third represent management.

At Motorola, teams take over very short-term planning, letting supervisors extend their planning focus over the long term. (Vice President Barten's description of who does what in planning is outlined in Chapter 5.)

• *Participate in setting their own goals.* In Motorola's Cellular Products Division, teams and management work together to set goals. It's up to the teams to determine how to accomplish them.

• *Participate in hiring.* At Northern Telecom, employee representatives sit in on hiring interviews and take the information they learn back to their teams. The team tallies up points on a tally sheet, and management does the same. Both sheets are used to make hiring decisions. As the teams mature, they take on even greater responsibility. The company has begun to train workers in the legal aspects of interviewing and hiring, and some employees have taken the lead in conducting hiring interviews. Eventually, Smith expects that the teams will conduct interviews without having management representatives present.

At Titeflex, teams have gone a step further and participate in hiring technical support people such as engineers. In some cases, Roberts prescreens technical hirees, meeting potential candidates for half an hour. Then the team interviews the leading candidates. The selection is made by consensus. A team convinced Roberts to change his mind about one choice. "They were right," he says.

Responsibilities of Mature Teams

Most teams wait until they are fully mature to take on the most sensitive personnel issues and big-number financial decisions. Teams are fully self-directed when they:

• *Determine their own overtime needs.* A Motorola manager recalls, "Someone asked me if our sector manager had released decision-making authority to me on whether a group worked overtime. In reality, the people on the manufacturing floor make that decision. They also participate in determining what has to be built to meet customer demands, costs, et cetera, so they can see whether overtime is needed or not."

In other companies, an in-between stage exists in which teams still do not enjoy full autonomy on overtime. At GE's Plant III in Lynn, teams monitor their own overtime, says Harding, but the decision to schedule overtime is a joint one involving teams and management.

• *Conduct performance appraisals.* Bill Crockett of Texas Instruments says teams have conducted annual peer appraisals for two years at the Fabrication Shop in Sherman, Texas. At Honeywell Commercial Flight Systems in Coon Rapids, Minnesota, a pilot team took over performance appraisals for its group earlier than teams do in most companies. They developed their own procedures and designed their own forms, which they sent to customers as well as team members. Two team members delivered the compilation of inputs to the individual being appraised, with a facilitator present to assist in a discussion of the results.

• *Discipline team members around performance problems.* This is one of the toughest issues for teams to face. Crockett says that all his plant's teams aren't up to this level yet, but some are taking on member performance issues. Several teams have given written guidance to members who have violated the plant's clear-cut attendance policy.

4

What Teams Need

Even in their early stages of development, teams take on many of the tasks that have kept supervisors busy throughout the history of modern industry. By the time they reach full maturity, they are managing themselves fully. Are they therefore totally self-sufficient? And if they don't need managing, what do they need?

As they make the transition into self-management, team members need the tools to do for themselves what management used to do for them. These tools include skills and knowledge, access to people and information from which they had previously been shut out, and the self-confidence to believe that they can solve problems that often stymied those trained and experienced in scientific management.

Team members need training in one another's tasks. Cross-functional flexibility is one of the basics that bolsters team members' quick response to challenges. Teams also need training in management functions. This training succeeds best when it is delivered in a combination of classroom education and on-the-job coaching. Many team-based organizations designate formal team roles — such as leader, recognizer, and communicator — which rotate periodically. To assume team roles, members need training in, among other things, facilitating meetings, recognizing and rewarding team members' accomplishments, promoting quality and safety, and communicating effectively.

To accomplish the best results, teams need to know not just what to do but why tasks need to be done. "We have to give them the vision, tell them why the company is doing this," asserts Bill Crockett of Texas Instruments. Teams need to know the direction the company is taking if they are to align their efforts with organizational objectives.

To make the best business decisions, teams need information about factors such as the life cycle of a product or service, marketing data, and cost data, things that in the past were often considered too proprietary for production workers, says Motorola Vice President Patty Barten. Michelle Thomas, a production manager at Motorola, illustrates with an example from her operation: "Say a person wants to change a part to make it easier to insert on the wave line [where operators insert parts that can't be put in by machine]. But the supervisor may know that the part is being phased out or that the life cycle [of the product] isn't long enough to justify the engineering effort." A team with access to information can itself make the appropriate decision about changing the part.

Confronted with tough business decisions or with interpersonal conflict within the team, members may need guidance or just a sounding board—someone who can ask, "Have you looked at the situation from this point of view? Have you covered all the bases, examined all the options?"

And sometimes, they do need someone to solve a problem that's beyond their reach. One Motorola team got an order for seventy units that were to go to Japan. After the parts for the units arrived, the customer altered the order. Stuck with all that excess material, the team went to the supervisor for guidance. The supervisor arranged for it to be used by other teams within the division to fill other orders.

Some issues arise that are too sensitive for teams—new ones, at least—to tackle. At Honeywell Commercial Flight Systems, managers meet to rank workers as part of the process for determining compensation. At first, says Organization Development Specialist Brenda Dietrich, the company's new teams thought they could send members to represent them at these meetings, but everyone soon realized that this wasn't feasible, and the coach took on that responsibility. Members also often feel uncomfortable discussing their conflicts with other workers within the team and prefer to report such problems to a coach.

Teams often need someone to run interference with upper management or with outside stakeholders. Sometimes, for example, says Barten of Motorola, production teams can't fulfill requirements because they can't get the necessary materials. "They may need help getting outside suppliers to be a little more creative in getting parts to us."

Sometimes it takes a little muscle to get a team member what he or she deserves. Team Manager Dave Litwin of Titeflex had some arguing to do to get holiday pay and a turkey for a retiree who had come back to work on a temporary basis. "Ten years ago," he admits ruefully, "I'd have felt good about not getting her a turkey. I would have saved the company $3.00." (But that was back during the days, when, as Titeflex managers like to say, they were members of the Evil Empire.)

Teams also need a link to other teams. Cell leaders at GE's Plant III sit down prior to each shift with representatives of all the teams to discuss what's in the shop and to determine if they need to share staff to fill orders on time. At Titeflex, Litwin meets three times a week with representatives of all teams to pass on company news as well as to share where all the teams stand regarding key result areas, such as customer satisfaction, work in progress, and new orders.

Sometimes, teams need gentle reminders to stay within the guidelines and rules they have set for themselves. In Wilma Weed's office at Bell Atlantic, teams have self-imposed agreements on points such as how long meetings may run and how many members must be present for a quorum. "Sometimes," she says, "I have to restrain them from saying, 'Oh, well, let's go ahead and decide this anyway.'"

Especially as teams form, members often need encouragement to take on the responsibilities and perceived risks of self-management. "The population wants rules and boundaries," says Karen Page of Texas Instruments. "They are uncomfortable with the increased responsibilities we are transferring to them. They are constantly begging us for rules. We tell them, 'You don't need rules. Make the decision for yourself.'"

Along with encouragement, team members may need to be challenged to keep taking the next step in teaming. Joan Clarke, a Motorola supervisor, had two workers on one line who constantly outperformed other team members. When they told Clarke, "We just beat so-and-so's record," her response (along with acknowledgment of their accomplishment) was, "Okay, why aren't you helping them to beat your record?" With her prodding, they found satisfaction in sharing, rather than hoarding, their winning techniques. One of those hyperspeed workers, Diane Lewis, is now a supervisor in the same division and a staunch supporter of empowered teams.

Finally, even mature teams need champions for the team system. Even at Titeflex, which has been so revitalized by self-directed work teams that it has become a model for other companies, Operations Manager Kevin Roberts contends that "this company has about ten cheerleaders for teams. Without them, the company would revert to its old style in a year."

Ensuring that all the teams' needs are met is the team coach's responsibility.

5

What Coaches Do

On the surface, the coach's job can look deceptively simple after teams have taken over many of the traditional management tasks. "Some guys think I'm a great politician," jokes Bill Harding of GE. "My job consists of going around and talking to people."

Unlike a politician, however, Harding is not lining up support for himself and his own agenda. As he makes his rounds, his sole purpose is to help others. "In GE," he explains, "we've always done a real good job of managing the business, but we haven't always done such a good job in helping people."

Patty Barten at Motorola likens the team coach's job to that of an air traffic controller. "Air traffic controllers don't tell the plane how to load and unload, its direction, or how to fly. Like controllers, our supervisors make sure there is coordination. They make sure people have information so they don't intersect where they shouldn't or go off in a nonproductive direction."

To help people, guide teams through takeoff and landing, and keep them from bumping into each other, coaches perform a number of functions. (A summary of coaches' functions appears in Figure 5–1.)

1. *Coaches build teams.* Teams are groups of people working together and helping each other achieve a common goal. A team doesn't happen just because you pull together a number of individuals and give them the team label. Bill Crockett of Texas Instruments discovered that early on. "We had people here doing the same thing for twenty years," he

Figure 5–1. What coaches do.

---

* Build teams
* Provide vision
* Transfer management responsibilities to teams
* Facilitate external relationships
* Provide resources
* Plan longer term
* Support team members' career development
* Participate in teams of their own

---

recalls. "Some people said they didn't want any part of this team thing."

Coaches arrange for training in team building and encourage members to apply that training back on the job. They also provide training and on-the-job coaching to help members perform their team roles. (At Bell Atlantic, these team-support functions are called "wheel roles." Texas Instruments calls them "star points"; teams in Bill Crockett's unit, for example, have six: coordinator, scheduler, quality star point, safety star point, training star point, and cost star point. Other Texas Instruments teams may have more or fewer star points, depending on the needs of the team.)

Since roles within the team rotate, members are learning new skills almost constantly. Team members therefore require ongoing support from the team coach. Wanda Vinson, team developer at Bell Atlantic, says one of her major tasks is developing every wheel role to its fullest potential. That can mean working with a team leader (comparable to the coordinator at Texas Instruments) to determine what the team needs to do to reach the next level of team development. It can mean helping the quality leader analyze what the team has attained, what goals it can set, and what action plans it needs to reach those goals.

Helping people develop the skills they need to perform their team roles often involves learning along with them. At Texas Instruments, Pete Keller uses the role of safety star point as an example: "Say someone wants to be a star point for safety. The facilitator helps find the training and learns along with the person." The facilitator must learn the new role because he or she is expected to be a mentor as well as a training coordinator.

Developing team roles can also mean providing vigilant oversight, especially when a member fails to meet the responsibilities of a role. "My recognition leader is constantly saying, 'I'm not a recognizer,'" Vinson relates. "I think she took the role because she saw it as easy. But I see it as an all-the-time job. I tell her you have to go look for things to recognize. A couple of days ago, I went to her and pointed out three small things people needed pats on the back for."

Coaches also support team development by mediating conflict within teams and helping team members learn to trust one another. In fact, without consistent coaching of this nature there is a strong chance teams won't jell. "I'm their third team developer in less than a year," Bell Atlantic's Krissan Zoby says of one of her teams, explaining why this team was not doing well. The team attributed its problems to lack of trust among its members. Zoby, in the Consumer Sales office in Virginia Beach, Virginia, works on the trust issue by encouraging team members to voice their feelings. "I've helped them express their feelings openly and honestly without being judgmental. I show them they can disagree and still move on."

2. *Coaches provide vision.* In a job that is often described as working for the teams, rather than the reverse, coaches take a leadership role in developing a vision of where the team is heading. Kevin Roberts at Titeflex says that Team Manager Litwin "implants a vision of where we want to go and rallies people to see that vision, identify team goals, and make the decision to 'reach go.'"

"The real challenge is to provide direction," says Barten of Motorola. The task is to clarify "the type of customer we're going after, what's important to customers, the margin we're going to operate on, the quality and cycle time we're going to hold you accountable for"—but not how to do the work, she stresses.

3. *Coaches transfer management responsibilities to teams.* It's not enough just for supervisors to let go, although for many supervisors even that is hard. The coach's work lies in the many tasks necessary to ensure teams' success.

Coaches prepare teams to take on their new responsibilities. They arrange training for team members in both business and interpersonal skills, and they follow up with on-the-job training to support people in applying what they have learned. Tom Howes, teaming process manager in Texas Instruments' Lewisville Center for Excellence, stresses the critical nature of this aspect of the coach's role: "Let's say I bring in a consultant on human resource training, who teaches people soft skills. Then the employees come back into the workplace. What I get out of that is awareness training—but we all tend to revert to kind as soon as pressure hits. Coaches have to be capable of teaching people to apply training day in and day out."

As teams assume new responsibilities, coaches pave their way through the minefield of relationships, regulations, and systems through which they have to maneuver to get work done. Where teams are not yet the norm throughout the organization, this is an especially large part of the coach's role. "We're still in the old environment," says Zoby of Bell Atlantic, "so when they run into a roadblock I negotiate things."

Even in an organization of mature teams, coaches need to step in when issues with other departments arise, although they probably act more as facilitators and guides and less as problem solvers. Joan Clarke of Motorola illustrates with a problem around financial reporting. "If there's an issue with finance," she points out, "the financial people are going to contact the supervisor to get it straightened out. The supervisor needs to facilitate a group meeting, help the team members understand the problem, and show them where to get the information they need to solve it."

Sometimes, coaches have to overcome team members' resistance toward taking on some of the less pleasant management tasks. Page at Texas Instruments describes a situation in her plant where the administration star points handle much of the labor relations. A person who needs to take a day off calls the administrative star point. "Under our pay-for-performance system, nonattendance hurts," says Page, "so we encouraged the administrative star points to ask people questions like: 'Are you going to make up the time? Are you sure you can't come in, and do what else you need to do after work?' Some of them said they didn't want to do that; they wanted to give that responsibility back to us. Some of the business unit managers were willing, but I insisted, 'No, we can't let them give up.'"

4. *Coaches facilitate external relationships.* Fred Eintracht, who pioneered empowered work teams at Texas Instruments' Defense Systems and Electronics Group, says that transferring responsibilities is the easy part; the hard part is dealing with the social aspects and relationships. That's where the mettle of the coach — or facilitator, to use Texas Instruments' terminology — is really tested.

At Titeflex, the union's chief steward, Ralph Galarneau, remembers not long ago when "lots of people couldn't even leave the department without a note from the supervisor." No wonder, then, that until they become members of SDWTs, many workers are totally unprepared to communicate on business issues with other departments, customers, and vendors. Not only do they lack the right contacts; they often must deal with people who are used to talking only to employees with fancy titles and who consider workers presumptuous if they initiate calls.

When teams are new, coaches may have to serve as their main link to the outside. Chuck Stridde, director of employee and labor relations at Northern Telecom and formerly with Saturn, gives some examples. Coaches at Saturn, he says, help deal with problems every day that require teams to reach out beyond themselves. If there's a product problem, for example, the coach may need to contact product engineering to bring help in. If there's a problem with a supplier — perhaps the trucks break down — the coach plays the lead role.

To help team members build their own links to outside

stakeholders, coaches guide them through channels, make introductions, and educate outsiders on the workers' new roles. Says Weed at Bell Atlantic, "We work to give them control over things they are responsible for." When her teams of service representatives took on billing responsibilities, they ran up against resistance from customers, who were used to dealing directly only with marketing people. Not only did Weed sit with each service rep as the rep made each collection call; before each call she contacted the customer's marketer and said, "From here on we're responsible for contacting customers about billing. Please call your customer and say we'll be handling this."

At GE, Harding's workers were frustrated as they tried to produce cooling plates from what seemed like an unmanufacturable design—an obstacle over which the workers had no control. "That's where our job came in," says Harding. "We brought in a design engineer. He sat down with our people, and they identified the characteristics our guys were having a devil of a time with. They examined the tolerances the guys were questioning." Between them, the workers and the engineer resolved the problems within a few months.

Coaches also facilitate communication among teams. Says Stridde, "Teams make a lot of decisions about how work gets done, but this gets tricky when they are trying to make a decision that affects other teams. The adviser, or coach, serves as a leader of discussion among teams, using consensus methodology."

Finally, coaches are the conduit to the next level in the organization. They bring information from upper management and represent their teams to the management team.

5. *Coaches provide resources.* These may include materials, time, skills training, or outside expertise. When Weed's teams took on billing, it was her responsibility to make sure they had all the tools they needed to do the job. She and another team developer arranged for the teams to get skills training—after confirming with team members that they needed it.

Figure 5–2. Changes in time frame for planning.

Planning	Immediate (Focus: What to Produce)	Few Months to Year (Focus: What to Produce Plus Capital Needs)	Long-range
Traditional	Supervisor	Management	Top mgt
Teams	Employees	Supervisor	Management

At GE, the cell leaders worked to break down the maintenance bureaucracy that resulted in delays of a week in getting something fixed. Now Plant III has its own maintenance department. When something breaks, "they just go grab a guy to get it fixed," Harding says.

6. *Coaches do longer-term planning.* When SDWTs take over the week-to-week planning for how work gets done, coaches plan for a longer time frame than supervisors in traditional settings.

When the supervisor becomes a coach, planning responsibilities change, states Barten of Motorola, from looking at what gets built today to considering "where you are going to take the business for the rest of the year." This change in time frame is shown in Figure 5–2.

7. *Coaches support the career development of team members.* The biggest challenge for the supervisor/coach, says Thomas of Motorola, is fostering "growth of people, giving them opportunities to learn new things, go into different departments."

She elaborates with an illustration from her own plant experience: "Operators get very good at running their machines. When they express a desire to move, the supervisor is confronted with a problem. If you take operators off machines they know, you open yourself up to production issues."

What changes the supervisor's outlook, explains Thomas, is the responsibility for longer-term planning. "When supervisors were held accountable for today, this week, they made those kinds of decisions based on: What do I have to turn out today? When they are held accountable for a year, they start to see the advantages of more people getting more exposure."

But it's not just the old-school supervisor who resists job changes, as Page of Texas Instruments has found out. Sometimes it's the workers themselves. As she has encouraged workers to develop new skills, some of them have resisted, claiming that they were hired just to build boards. Her response: "People were hired twenty years ago to bc key punch operators. You could be the best key punch operator in the country now, but I still wouldn't need you. We don't have the luxury of the status quo. What happens if we don't need electronic assemblers anymore?"

8. *Coaches participate in teams of their own.* In many organizations, the team organization extends beyond workers to include management as well. At Bell Atlantic, the team developers form a team that has all the same wheel roles that exist in the worker teams. Vinson's sensitivity to the needs of her SDWT's recognition leader was heightened by the fact that she herself was recognition leader on the team developer team.

Although coaches' responsibilities are fairly consistent among most organizations that employ SDWTs, the coach job description is neither universal nor static. Depending on the organization, coaches take on other responsibilities as well, especially when teams are new. They may continue to conduct performance appraisals, handle discipline problems, and occasionally even pitch in and work along with the team members. Some of the tasks that are commonly assigned to coaches of new teams are shown in Figure 5–3.

Confronting Challenges and Unresolved Issues

Because teams are still new in most organizations and because in many cases they have been created in response to

Figure 5–3. Transition role of the coach.

---

* Teach members to understand the business
* Participate in and teach conflict resolution
* Help determine training and educational requirements
* Practice staying neutral and two-way communication
* Eliminate or actively transfer supervisory responsibility
* Serve as leader/mediator/arbitrator as required
* Gain and maintain open environment based on trust and mutual respect
* Transfer specialized knowledge
* Teach how to prioritize goals and organize ideas into tangible outputs
* Teach team how to share skills, information, accountability, and responsibility
* Teach behaviors and consequences

---

business crises, team coaches often work in an unsettled environment. The new team structure exists uneasily side by side with pesky remnants of the traditional hierarchy and old systems. To further confound the situation, new, unanticipated issues can rear their heads, such as:

* *Push/pull relationship between team and coach.* Guarding their new power, teams sometimes hold coaches at arm's length, yet expect them to be deeply involved when problems arise. At the request of her teams, Page of Texas Instruments has an office half a wing away from where they work. The teams were uncomfortable having her in a position to watch over them constantly, fearing that she would slip back into the traditional supervisor role. And yet, when she is stuck in her office, caught up in paperwork, their cry is, "Why aren't you out here?"

* *Use of traditional measurements of performance.* Coaches have difficulties motivating team members to work in a new mode when they are still being evaluated according to traditional standards. At GE's Plant III, both the plant manager, Jerry Labadini, and Harding, a cell leader, note that traditional efficiency measurements undermine their efforts to

encourage teams of machine operators to take on the whole business of manufacturing a product. "Operators here do a lot of things beyond running machines," points out Harding. "They also oil machines, pick up materials, participate in environmental health and safety committees, and a host of other activities." But their efficiency measurements dub those activities "idle time."

Many Teams or One?

Call it the postteam syndrome, perhaps. Whether they are fine-tuning the team system or riding the next wave, Page and her colleagues at Texas Instruments' McKinney Board Shop are focusing now on the whole plant as one team. "We had strong, autonomous, stand-alone teams, but sometimes the right decision for the team was not the right decision for the shop," she explains. "We said, 'Cut that. We want one strong team.'"

The plant still has small teams executing product lines. However, the focus is not just on the metrics of individual teams but on how the teams fit into the "jigsaw puzzle of the McKinney Board Shop." Page admits that it's hard to be on a team of 170 people; some members saw the change as diminishing the powers of teams and were frustrated by what felt like two steps forward, one step back. "But the light bulbs are coming on," Page says. "It's pretty exciting stuff."

6

New Outlook

Making the transition from traditional supervisor to coach requires more than a new set of behaviors. To succeed, and to relish the change, demands a totally different outlook. For a coach, the intrinsic rewards—the enjoyment of work—come from knowing you've helped others develop to the full extent of their potential. Rewards come from increasing the value you add to the organization by replicating your skills among many; from watching an individual's good idea blossom into the brilliant achievement of a team as everyone contributes; and from experiencing the power of a shift from an "I" focus to a "we" focus, not by subjugating the individual, but by nourishing the synergy generated by a group of multi-skilled individuals sharing a goal.

There's more than one route to the place where that outlook prevails. Patty Barten at Motorola had long cherished ideas about empowering workers. She got a chance to implement them fully when she went to work for a boss who had opened a new path by creating a team environment.

Kevin Roberts at Titeflex had a longer road to travel. Ralph Galarneau, the union chief steward, had once told a labor negotiator, "You get rid of Kevin and you'll have labor peace here for ten years."

"My learned style of management, from college and my mentors, was autocratic," Roberts admits. "As I started to experience different management styles in training sessions, I began to learn." Although apprehensive, he tried new things, and as they started to work, his attitude changed.

At Texas Instruments, the change was incremental. It started, relates Fred Eintracht, with moves to treat work more as a process than a series of tasks. This initial change led the company to give the people who did the work more responsibility for developing methodology. The results were impressive. As workers began making commitments to customers on costs and scheduling, they took ownership for fulfilling their promises. When the company employed just-in-time techniques, workers became much more active in areas that had been the responsibility of support operations, things like laying out workflow, once the exclusive domain of engineers. With this track record to convince them, Eintracht and other managers took the leap and began to experiment with true self-directed teams.

At the same company, Tom Howes's conversion had more of a "eureka" flavor. He experienced what he calls a "significant emotional event" that spurred his transformation from traditional manager to champion of teams. As the outlook for companies dependent on federal defense contracts began to dim in the late 1980s, Texas Instruments started to investigate other markets for its defense systems unit. When he visited companies in commercial business, Howes heard talk about downsizing and rightsizing and about the need to cut away parts of the business that added costs without adding value.

What stuck in his mind was, "What if that happened to us?" He concluded that he and other managers were adding costs, not value, because they hadn't made people capable of taking on a multiplicity of functions. His pursuit of a system to make people capable and to empower them to use their capabilities fully led him to embrace self-directed work teams.

For all these managers, the switch from directing and controlling in a traditional hierarchy to supporting empowered workers in a team environment has been much more than an adjustment in methodology. Each has experienced a change in mind-set like that outlined in Figure 6–1.

Figure 6–1. Mind-set changes.

Traditional Manager	Coach
Lectures	Listens
Absorbs energy	Supplies energy
Provides direction	Provides focus
Absorbs information	Provides information
Controls	Influences
Requires risk	Shares risk
Seeks directed glory	Seeks reflected glory
Vertical orientation	Horizontal orientation
Recognizes what's wrong	Recognizes what's right
Values likeness	Values difference
Involves	Evolves

Source: Tom Howes, Teaming Process Manager, Lewisville Center for Excellence, Defense Systems and Electronics Group, Texas Intruments. Used with permission.

Working Through Influence

Most supervisors have invested years in learning their business. No doubt they, more than anyone, know what needs to be done in most situations. Stripped of the authority to tell people what to do, are the new supervisors-turned-coaches powerless if they see teams making mistakes or failing to perform critical tasks?

Not to hear them tell it.

"On the organization chart, nobody reports to me, yet I can get anything done that needs to be done," says Joe Reece, production control supervisor at GE's Plant III in Lynn. Reece doesn't work through authority, the power base granted by the organization; he works through influence, a power base earned by demonstrating expertise, trustworthiness, and respect for others. When your source of power is authority, others pay attention to you because they have to; when your power base is influence, others pay attention to you because they want to.

Demonstrating Expertise

In a traditional organization, supervisors have most of the knowledge and information. Often, they keep that information close to the chest. They tell workers what to do, but not why, nor how it fits in with what others do. Workers view them less as a source of information than as a source of marching orders.

At Titeflex, people describe how it used to be, and how it's changed. "We used to hide the numbers from employees," says Kevin Roberts. "Now every employee has access to all financial information."

Ralph Galarneau, the chief union steward, explains the impact. "It used to be that the supervisor would be screaming and yelling. Only he had the pressure. Now we know the good news and the bad. You see stress on people's faces to make due dates."

To build influence, coaches demonstrate expertise by sharing it, by communicating all they can learn about the goals and plans of the organization, by explaining the reasons behind management decisions, by contributing new technical information when they have it, and by coaching others in the skills that they have and the others don't. In a team environment, coaches offer their expertise generously, but without intimidation. Tim Smith of Northern Telecom has provided his team with a form to use to track quality problems, but the team is under no obligation to use it. "They can use it or not," he says. "As a team they can do a new form. They can overrule any of my decisions." He's comfortable with this arrangement. As he sees it, his job is to give the team members encouragement and to work with them, not to insist that they do things his way.

Trustworthiness

In fact, whether or not they do things exactly his way, the members of Smith's teams do pay heed to his ideas. They do it because "we've gotten to the point where people do trust us," he avows. In a team environment, where you can't say, "Listen up, folks, we're going to do this my way," only coaches who are trusted get a chance even to demonstrate their expertise, let alone use their influence to get work done.

Building trust, Smith has found, requires coaches to:

- Communicate frequently, telling the bad with the good
- Obtain top management support for team decisions
- Pay attention to and implement team ideas, and let team members see what you do
- Accept some bad decisions; otherwise, he adds, "You won't get good ones."

Crockett of Texas Instruments shares a similar list of trust-building techniques:

- Walk the talk.
- Listen to team members, and really follow up.
- Show evidence that you are helping.
- Recognize when the team's performance is good; tell members when performance is not good, but . . .
- Don't beat them up for failure in a learning situation; instead, show them where they might do better next time.
- Be the team's advocate.

Perhaps the most important thing to remember about developing trustworthiness is that trust is a two-way street. You earn it by extending it to others. When a team member, accompanied by Galarneau, brought a written grievance to Roberts of Titeflex, Roberts asked, "What do you feel is right?" As they pondered, he simply signed his name and told the employee and Galarneau to fill in what they felt was right. In the new culture, he says, "You have to trust your teammates 100 percent."

When Reece of GE says he can get anything done that needs to be done, the reason is that he trusts the workers at Plant III to know what to do and how to do it. "If I say we have to get that part on an airplane by 2 o'clock, they already know that. People here understand what has to be done," he states with complete confidence.

Respect for Others

Of course, the coach won't always agree with the team's approach to getting a task done or solving a problem. What then? "Whether you agree or not, you let them do it," insists Barten of Motorola. "You've got to trust and respect people's ability."

Showing respect also means being open to the team's feedback regarding your actions, even if it's negative. "Many of these people have taken me for a walk in the parking lot when I've made a mistake," says Bill Harding of GE. "We have mutual respect for each other. I have undying respect for the people in the shop."

Clearly, having influence doesn't mean always getting your own way. It does mean that, like Reece, you can get anything done that needs to be done.

7

New Skills

To achieve in any field of endeavor, an individual needs a philosophy, a source of power, and the ability to perform the work. For coaching teams, the heart of the philosophy is that value lies in making others capable. (See Figure 7–1.) The source of power is influence. And the ability includes a set of skills coaches need to perform their tasks. These skills are listed in Figure 7–2.

These skills include:

1. *Listening*. To a person, everyone with responsibilities for coaching teams puts listening at the top of the skills list. Having learned to do much more telling than listening as they moved up in the traditional organization, they now concentrate on listening actively, empathetically, respectfully, and without passing judgment.

They listen when workers propose new ideas, such as taking a product made primarily for aircraft engines and selling it to a motorcycle manufacturer. As a result, a new market opens up.

They listen when team members complain that one of their coworkers isn't carrying her share of the load. Just by listening, a coach can serve as a mirror that reveals to the grumbling workers their own responsibility for handling the problem.

They listen when employees take them "to the parking lot." And if, being human, they slip back into the old "boss" role and start giving directions or making decisions that are no longer theirs to make, they pay heed when team members remind them that they've overstepped their bounds.

Figure 7–1. Prerequisites for success.

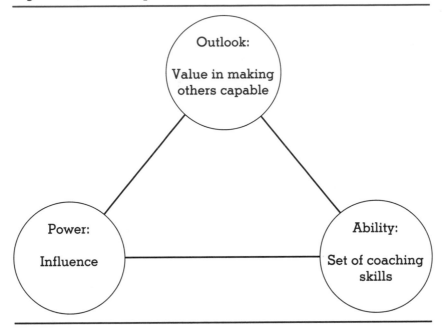

Figure 7–2. Essential skills for team coaches.

* Listening
* Communicating
* Advocating
* Team building
* Facilitating decision making
* Training
* Educating
* Mentoring

They learn to listen between the lines to stay abreast of current problems and to anticipate upcoming ones so that they are ready to provide assistance when needed.

Just by listening, they learn, they help others learn, and they both show and earn respect.

2. *Communicating.* Coaches must know how to communicate, not only in meetings, but also one-to-one, out in the

workplace. Bill Crockett of Texas Instruments stresses the importance of ensuring that everyone receives a complete, consistent message. He was first struck by the volume of misinformation circulating among workers when he began communicating with them directly instead of going through supervisors. "I really hadn't been aware of how much — or how little — communication there was. It really brought home the need to communicate clearly."

Now, he communicates directly with team representatives at steering team meetings, where the group discusses such things as the status of work, what's coming down the line, and policy changes. The representatives go back and share what they've talked about with their fellow team members. But even that's not enough, Crockett says. "Many times after we have steering committee meetings and go over things, I go out on the shop floor and discover all the workers haven't heard what's been discussed. Things have been miscommunicated or not passed down." That's why he makes a point of communicating informally with each team daily.

3. *Advocating.* Coaches need the skill and the passion to make a cogent case, often in the face of indifference, skepticism, or overt opposition, for the team system, for team innovations, and for the rights of individual team members.

If, as the team champions at Titeflex predict, it takes two generations for a team system to become imbedded in the culture of the organization, there's going to be a continued need for advocacy just to keep teams alive, even when their results are positive. Advocating for the team system is part public relations — publicizing team success to high-level decision makers, to internal and external customers, and even to team members themselves. It's part rebuttal, always being ready to counter the arguments of those who, out of expediency, ignorance, or self-interest, fight to turn back the clock and regain control for the elite. It's part vigilance, withstanding the natural forces that through omission, rather than commission, would return the system to the status

Figure 7–3. Linkages and interdependencies.

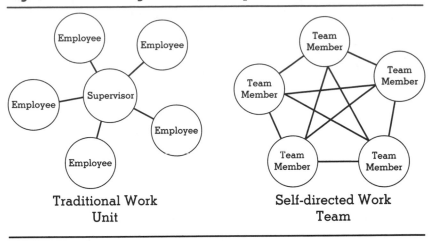

Traditional Work
Unit

Self-directed Work
Team

quo ante. And it's part damage control, because teams, be-ing new, will make mistakes (why not?—hierarchies do and they've been around for centuries), but mistakes can be learning experiences, not excuses to chuck the system.

Without an advocate, the best ideas that come out of teams may never come to fruition.

4. *Team building.* On the surface, the biggest difference between a traditional work unit and a self-directed work team is the presence or absence of a supervisor. But the big-gest underlying difference is in how team members relate to one another (see Figure 7–3).

A traditional work unit is held together by the relation-ship between the supervisor and each individual in the unit. Often individual employees work independently of each other, knowing little about each other's work. A self-directed work team can't operate that way. Without the glue of a su-pervisor, what keeps it from splintering and falling apart are team members' commitment to team goals, their willing-ness to work together and their ability to do so without trip-ping all over each other, and their confidence in one another's expertise, judgment, and good intentions. Only such a team can succeed in managing itself and its business over the long term.

Wilma Weed of Bell Atlantic says that on one of her teams, at least three people have very strong personalities. In the beginning they did excellent work and preferred to do it on their own. Excellent or not, operating that way, the team could never have survived. With Weed's help, "the team has brought them into the fold. They have learned to use everybody's strengths. For example, one person has better letter-writing skills, another is good at collecting. They've stopped thinking 'me, me, me.' Now they think 'us.'"

Building a team like that takes a lot of skill, and much of the responsibility falls to the team coach. Bill Harding of GE describes the skill of team building as "taking five or six people of different cultural backgrounds and getting them to understand each other and perform as a team."

5. *Facilitating decision making.* Coaches and team members both need training in group decision making and in consensus building. Most SDWTs have team leaders (or coordinators, as they are called at Texas Instruments) who chair team meetings. So it is usually not appropriate for team coaches to take over and formally facilitate sessions in which problems are worked through and decisions made. But team coaches do need skills to support team leaders, working one on one with them in advance of team meetings and giving them feedback afterward.

Wanda Vinson at Bell Atlantic turns postmeeting assessments into opportunities for development for team leaders. When a team fails to make a decision, she says, "usually the team leader saw what happened but just didn't know how to handle it. My job is giving feedback and coaching, asking, 'At what point could you have brought closure?' Usually they know but are afraid or uncomfortable going up against a team member."

When the ordered processes of team decision making and consensus building break down and the loudest—rather than the most learned—voices start to take over, there are ways that a team coach can skillfully intercede from the sidelines without usurping the role of meeting facilitator. When Karen Page of Texas Instruments thinks a decision is being determined by the strongest personality, rather than by the best ideas, she voices the point of view that is going unheard. She explains, "I've got some strong personalities and some not so strong. The strong ones are sometimes overwhelming. We react to loud people, but we can't always hear the quiet ones over the din. I'm careful about making sure one constituency doesn't get the floor too long. I may float what I think is the quiet person's point of view."

What if the team makes a decision that the coach thinks is a bad or a hasty one? A skilled coach asks some leading questions to encourage the team to broaden its thinking or look at the problem in another way. "When we feel they might be heading down the wrong path," says Harding of GE, "we ask questions like, 'Why do you think that's right? Did you look into this, think about that?'" Sometimes, he adds, when you ask those questions, you find out they did indeed think about all those things and their decision is the right one.

Even in SDWTs, all decisions aren't made by teams; individuals are called upon to make decisions for themselves all day long. But it is hard for individuals to break a deeply ingrained habit of taking problems to the supervisor for solutions. New supervisors-turned-coaches can expect team members to continue to look to them for decisions. Not only do coaches need to avoid the temptation to take the easy way out and just tell workers what to do; they need skills to guide workers to make well-reasoned decisions for themselves. Again, this usually involves asking probing questions.

"I don't give them the answer even if I know it," stresses Vinson. "I ask, 'How would you handle it?' I encourage them to look beyond right now. 'What are the consequences? What would be the result?'"

Part of facilitating decision making by others can be shoring up their confidence in their ability to make decisions for themselves. When workers come to Dave Litwin of Titeflex for a decision, he may ask, "How many years' experience do you have?" Since the answer is usually a number like twelve, he urges them to look for answers in their own experience. He'll ask what they did last time in a similar situation. Usually, after they tell him, he assures them, "That sounds good to me."

In fact, Litwin maintains that one of his best assets as a team manager/coach is that he's not an expert at the technical and mechanical aspects of the job. "So I don't run out and tell people how to do things," he explains.

6. *Training.* Although SDWTs take over many of the training responsibilities of traditional supervisors, team coaches still find plenty of opportunities to put their training skills to use. In fact, much of what they do is to provide on-the-job training, not so much in the technical aspects of the workers' jobs — usually the teams handle that — but in the new leadership, facilitation, interpersonal, and administrative tasks that fall to the workers as they become members of self-directed work teams. Training workers to handle their "wheel" or "star point" roles is a significant part of the team coach's job — even though a new coach who has just moved out of a traditional supervisor's job may be just one step ahead of the team members themselves in mastering the skills of participative management.

Extensive classroom training for new team members should be a given. Chuck Stridde, now with Northern Telecom, recalls that when Saturn set about to form teams out of experienced General Motors production workers, the company provided employees with upwards of three hundred hours of training, including training in both interpersonal and technical skills. But even when the organization provides classroom training for new team members, the job doesn't end there. Classrooms provide what Tom Howes of Texas Instruments calls "awareness training." To bring that to life, he asserts, "we have to have coaches who are capable of teaching people to apply their training day in and day out."

Furthermore, since team roles typically rotate, by the time new people take on the responsibilities of coordinator, scheduler, recognizer, or safety star point, most of what they learned in their initial training has been lost. They may get some cross-training from their predecessors in the team roles, but it's the coach's responsibility to see that each succeeding person takes the new role and runs with it.

7. *Educating.* The most common way to differentiate between education and training is to explain education as teaching knowledge and training as teaching skills. People who work with SDWTs have refined that distinction. As Chief Steward Galarneau of Titeflex explains it, education teaches *why* and training teaches *how.* "If you tell them why," he goes on, "they might come up with a better idea for how to do it." He illustrates with an example from building: You can give people hammer and nails and show them how to fasten two boards together, or you can tell them why you want the boards together and see what solution they come up with.

Smith of Northern Telecom expresses a similar idea. "You train a dog to do something," he says. "You educate a person to know what to do."

Training is critical, but, Galarneau concludes, "if you educate people, they'll make better decisions on the floor."

8. *Mentoring.* Like training and educating, mentoring is a way to help others develop skills and confidence. Indeed, in order to do the job well, a mentor needs to be familiar with the skills of training and educating as well as those of listening and communicating. But mentoring involves more. Good mentors use their own experience and understanding of the organization—its people, processes, and products—to provide guidance for dealing with immediate issues, making decisions that will have positive long-term impact, establishing and pursuing career goals, and generally operating effectively within the culture and structure of the organization. They model, demonstrate, and explain attitudes and behaviors that are appropriate in the organization and in the particular situation.[1]

---

1. Adapted from G. Shea, *Mentoring: Helping Employees Reach Their Full Potential* (New York: American Management Association, 1994).

In addition to staying in regular contact with those they are mentoring and providing support and encouragement, mentors introduce their protégés to other people who might provide information or help them to clarify and attain their goals. To some degree, at least, mentors put their own credibility and reputation on the line to pave the way for their mentees.

Mentoring requires not only skill but commitment, dedication, and an ability to find enjoyment in helping others. In traditional hierarchies, most mentors concentrate their attention on one protégé at a time. Team coaches are called on to provide a comparable level of support and sponsorship to entire teams of people.

Empowerment Versus Abdication

Team coaches use all the skills discussed in the preceding section to one end: to develop empowered teams. But coaches also need another capability that may seem out of line with those we have discussed. They need to be able to intervene. They also need to be able to determine when an intervention is appropriate and what kind of intervention will support the goals of the organization and the team, while bolstering the team's ability to handle a similar situation on its own next time. In some cases, avoiding intervention isn't empowerment; it's abdication. It's giving the team enough rope to hang itself.

Smith of Northern Telecom uses backlog analysis as an example. Handling backlog is a team responsibility, but, he cautions, "If a team says, 'We're at 25 percent, but we can take it,' the coach may have to get in there and show them the impact of their decision." Notice that the intervention he calls for in this case isn't making the decision for the team but keeping the team on track by pointing out the consequences of a poor decision.

Pete Keller of Texas Instruments describes the art of intervention this way: "Let them make mistakes and not be punished for it. But stop them before making a big mistake."

Unfortunately, there's no exact science that differentiates between a mistake that's a worthwhile learning experience and one that's too big to allow. That judgment grows out of experience, intuition, business knowledge, and common sense.

Sometimes the best intentions can feel like desertion, rather than empowerment, when management imbues members of new teams with more responsibility than they are ready to assume. Vinson at Bell Atlantic tells how her first team leaders were overwhelmed by the volume of new information they were suddenly expected to understand, disseminate, and react to.

Initially, she recalls, the team leaders were asked to take on a lot of tasks for which the assistant manager had previously been responsible. For example, the team was being flooded with messages from management via the team leaders. Very quickly, team leaders were inundated with new information that the early team training had not addressed, such as announcements of corporate initiatives and concerns. Their reaction to these messages was, "What am I supposed to do with this?"

Vinson tells what happened: "The job was becoming very weighty for the team leaders. The feeling began to develop among them that they were taking on my job." They weren't equipped to handle the new pressures, and if the team leaders weren't effective, that lack of effectiveness had a ripple effect on the team; the team didn't get the information it needed to be effective.

"I had to go back to the source of this distribution, my manager," she continues, "and say, 'You're sending them information they can't handle right now. Filter it through me.'"

Vinson also realized that she too had overestimated the proper role of team leaders. "Initially," she says, "I saw their role to be handshaking with every other role on the team, partnering to the quality person, recognizer, communicator, et cetera. If the quality person was not making information available, I expected the team leader to touch base with that person to see what was getting in the way. If the recognition person wasn't recognizing anything, I thought the team leader would touch base and find out why."

Experience showed her that these expectations, far from being empowering, were overpowering. Now, she says, "I've taken back these developmental responsibilities."

She adds, "At first I saw myself interacting with the team leaders more than any other role. I hoped to get them to want to be more empowered, more accountable. Then I stepped back and asked myself, 'Wanda, are you really trying to clone them into you?'" Now she gives them the opportunity to be themselves and to take on responsibility at their own pace.

Training for Team Coaches

Where do coaches learn how to work through influence? Where do they get the training and coaching they need to develop the skills for the job? How do they acquire the judgment that helps them differentiate between empowering and abdicating?

At the very least, the coaches and managers interviewed for this book received first-class training in team building, problem solving, managing conflict, listening, giving feedback, and other interpersonal skills. The lucky ones also receive ongoing coaching from their managers, people like Barten and Thomas at Motorola and Jerry Labadini at General Electric.

At Texas Instruments, where some of the facilitators (as team coaches are called there) come from the ranks of hourly workers, there's a sprinkling, says Tom Howes, of "doctor's doctors"—people like Eintracht, Keller, and himself. These doctor's doctors teach facilitators not only coaching skills but also "how to think like business people, in terms of hours per system, for example, as well as costs and what makes on-time delivery."

There are no shortcuts. Says Howes, "You have to spend

Figure 7-4. Facilitator training.

SKILL	ACT AS CATALYST	COMMUNICATION	ADVISE/COACH	TEAMS AND CONFLICT	ASSIST IN METRIC DEPLOY	INFORMATION SYSTEMS	TRANSFER RESPONSIBILITY	ASSIST WITH MEETINGS	SUPPORT TEAM CONCEPT	KNOW PROCESS	KNOW PROBLEM SOLVING	TECHNICAL ENHANCEMENTS	BEHAVIORS/CONSEQUENCES	USE STATISTICAL TOOLS	UNDERSTAND OPERATIONS	TRANSFER SKILLS
(name)																
(name)																
(name)																
(name)																

COURSES   (For each category above, the matrix indicates one or more internal or outside course where skills can be learned.)

Source: Tom Howes, Teaming Process Manager, Lewisville Center for Excellence, Defense Systems and Electronics Group, Texas Instruments. Used with permission.

an inordinate amount of money and time up front on training people." To be successful, team coaches need the same
training and nurturing they give team members. Figure 7–4
illustrates the kind of training facilitators (coaches) get in
Howes's operation. It is a form used to track the training
each facilitator receives.

Part III

Coaching a Team to Self-Manage Its Work

When Bell Atlantic's Interexchange Carrier Service Center in Silver Springs, Maryland, made the decision to reorganize into self-directed work teams, some of its employees quickly latched onto the words "self-directed."

"At the start," recalls Team Developer Wilma Weed, "a lot of reps said, 'I am self-directed. Let me go ahead and do it.'" Although their enthusiasm was heartening, what it ignored was the fact that work does need to be managed. A self-directed work team is not a bunch of people doing their own thing. It is a group of people who work together to manage their work processes, solve their work problems, and run the team as a business.

In a traditional workplace, managers and supervisors perform these tasks. Unfortunately, in a hierarchy where people are accountable for their activities to those on the level above, not those on the level below, management tasks are almost invisible to employees—as long as they are done well. Done poorly, they are often much more apparent, which means employees charged with new management responsibilities often have a better grasp of what not to do than what to do.

If you are a team coach, you need to ensure that team members have the skills, tools, and resources to manage the work of the team. The next three chapters provide guidance for doing that.

8

Managing Processes and Mastering Skills

In their transition to self-management, teams usually begin by assuming responsibility for managing many of their own work processes. They may start by determining daily work to be done, assigning tasks, tracking production, and producing regular status reports. As the teams mature over months, they take on additional responsibilities until eventually they are developing and managing their own budgets and even purchasing raw materials or capital equipment.

At the same time, team members become responsible for assessing what skills are necessary to produce the team's products or services and to perform the ancillary tasks — such as measuring quality, maintaining equipment, and monitoring and improving safety and ergonomics — that are essential to the success of the team. As teams mature, it is up to them to ensure that team members have those skills.

Transferring Responsibility for Managing Work

Your job as a team coach is to ensure that team members have the information, training, guidance, and support they need to be successful. Here is a step-by-step process that will help you to achieve this goal:

1. Set up training for team members.
2. Reinforce training with coaching and immediate opportunities to apply the new knowledge and skills.

3. Create an atmosphere that encourages the application of new knowledge and skills learned.
4. Anticipate and deal with obstacles.
5. Monitor progress.
6. Provide feedback and ongoing support.
7. Recognize and reward accomplishments.

This process is based on the advice of managers and team coaches in organizations that have teams at various levels of maturity. You can adapt it to your situation by adjusting the emphasis you put on each step, depending upon variables such as the availability of other support services (e.g., a good training department), the existing skills of the team members, and their willingness to take the management baton and run with it.

Set Up Training for Team Members

Management at GE's Plant III restarted the entire plant from scratch when it closed the superautomated Factory of the Future in 1992 and reopened it a couple of months later as an operation built around self-directed work teams. When that happened, says Production Leader Joe Reece, "before anyone hit the shop, they got six weeks' training. This was a huge commitment." That was a long time for employees to sit in a classroom. Everyone got lessons in business issues, such as quality, statistical process control, how orders are placed, what makes the business win or lose, and why costs and overhead are important.

Most organizations don't have the luxury of closing shop and training everyone for teams at once. Most likely, the organization will provide some basic training for everyone before the switch to teams occurs, with extensive training still to come even as teams begin to take on management tasks. With so much work to do, you'll need to be diligent to ensure that training doesn't fall through the cracks. To do this:

Figure 8–1.   Work processes.

The list below includes processes used in a wide spectrum of workplaces. For your starter list, select those that are applicable to your teams.

- Managing work flow
- Scheduling work
- Assigning tasks
- Controlling costs
- Ordering supplies, equipment, and raw materials
- Consolidating orders with other departments
- Managing inventory
- Inspecting work
- Correcting errors
- Measuring production
- Measuring customer satisfaction
- Producing regular production reports
- Reviewing measurements and processes
- Managing special projects
- Identifying required job skills
- Measuring quality
- Maintaining equipment
- Monitoring and improving safety and ergonomics

• *Identify required knowledge and skills.* Get team members to list all the work processes required to get their product or service to its customer satisfactorily. To get them started, you might provide a list of universal processes, like that shown in Figure 8–1, and invite them to add others that are company- or team-specific.

• *Determine appropriate training methods, and identify sources.* You don't have to reinvent the wheel. Begin by checking with your company's training department for information about in-house courses and for referrals to outside vendors. Check with your peers in the organization for referrals to both internal and external programs. If you have no internal training resources or you need additional outside refer- ences, contact your industry associations, local universities or technical schools, and your peers in other companies. Ask for and check references for both internal and external programs. Get feedback from your team members on courses they have already attended.

Some of your training for new team members can be much less formal. You can follow the lead of Tim Smith of Northern Telecom and run a series of "developmental meetings" if you have the expertise and skills yourself, or you can pull together a group of experts from your own or other departments. At Northern Telecom these meetings were used to educate employees to understand the impact of costs and efficiency. Armed with this knowledge, says Smith, team members can measure their efficiency daily, in time to make necessary corrections if they've had a bad day, rather than wait for a monthly report.

Stay alert to team members' potential for conducting some of their own training. If you have a team member with demonstrated facilitation and coaching skills or the ability to create training materials, encourage her to put those talents to work. Weed of Bell Atlantic reports that her team members write a lot of their own training materials, especially since support staff positions have been reduced. She describes how "one of my service reps just trained three new people for three weeks on how to take and process a service order." The rep developed a binder and job aids and even scheduled the training room.

Determine where cross-training can work effectively to spread processes and skills throughout the team. "Cross-training—becoming multiskilled—is a fundamental of self-directed work teams," says Bill Crockett, Responsibility Center manager at Texas Instruments. "It makes people more valuable to the company."

Patty Barten, vice president of Motorola's Cellular Products Division, concurs. She describes as key having people cross-trained and certified in many skill bases. That way, she explains, "when a slowdown occurs in one business, they can switch to another."

Karen Page, business unit manager at Texas Instruments, gives a more immediate reason for cross-training. "We have some people who really hate doing one process or another. When we took the first step of giving them responsibility to make work assignments, everybody gravitated toward what they liked." That meant that some people grabbed the plum assignments and hung on to them. Inevitably, other people got stuck with tasks no one much wanted, and eventually, people began to grumble. So the team members made the decision to rotate jobs but found that in order to do so they needed to become fully cross-trained.

Cross-training can be a fallout of people working closely together. But it is more effective if the trainee learns from a master, who is proficient both at the work process and at one-on-one training. For some management processes, you may be the best on-the-job coach yourself; for other processes, team members can train each other. Figure 8–2 provides a step-by-step guide to one-on-one training that you or a skilled team member can apply.

Job aids are a good cross-training tool. Krissan Zoby of Bell Atlantic says that one of her teams has created small worksheets that break jobs down into their component steps. The worksheets are so specific that just by following them an untrained person can do parts of the jobs. The team members also use the worksheet for training one another on Saturdays, when work is slower and employees have more free time.

• *Schedule training, and follow up to ensure that it happens.* Unless your team has a training coordinator, scheduling and tracking training will probably be part of your job. If the team does have a designated training coordinator, you'll need to help the person develop a system for handling the responsibility. The first task is prioritizing training needs. To get the information you'll need:

— Determine whether the organization wants the teams to take over certain processes immediately, six months from now, a year from now. You'll need to know not only what the organizational directives are,

Figure 8–2.   Steps for one-on-one training.

1. Break the task down into its component steps. Spell out each step in detail. Nothing can be assumed or "go without saying." Have your task breakdown reviewed by someone else skilled in performing the task, and confirm it by having an unskilled person perform the task by following your list step by step.
2. Invite the trainee to describe—or better yet demonstrate—what he knows about the task.
3. Confirm the knowledge and skills the trainee already has. In the training, emphasize those aspects of the task that are unfamiliar to the trainee.
4. Demonstrate and describe the task step by step. You can do this in a training session or have the trainee observe you as you do real work.
5. Invite the trainee to question anything that is unclear.
6. If the task is complicated, demonstrate again.
7. Have the trainee perform the task. Give the trainee performance feedback (corrective and positive).
8. Have the trainee repeat any steps that caused problems. Give feedback and assistance.
9. When the trainee has correctly performed each step, have him repeat the entire task.
10. Observe the trainee's performance on the job. Give assistance as necessary: encourage the trainee to try what he thinks is right, but don't leave him floundering. Provide corrective feedback and positive reinforcement.

but whether they are negotiable if a team is more comfortable moving more slowly.

—Obtain the team members' preferences. When they review the list of work processes they are expected to manage, determine what order and timing they would prefer for assuming these tasks.

—Make your own assessment of the team's readiness.

—Identify the skills team members already have that would allow them to take over the management of a process immediately, without further training.

—Decide whether the entire team needs training in a

process or whether one person can be designated to manage it, allowing others to be trained later to take over as assignments are rotated. Managing quality, for example, is often a specified team role.

Armed with this analysis, you and the team members can determine which processes they will take over first and schedule training to correspond with those priorities.

To do that, you'll need a form for keeping records. A good model is the matrix that Tom Howes uses for facilitators at Texas Instruments' Lewisville Center for Excellence (see Figure 7–4). Down the left side of the form, list names of team members. Across the top, insert the work processes in the order in which the team expects to assume these tasks. Across the bottom, insert the appropriate course or other learning experience for each process.

Howes suggests putting a circle in each square as team members demonstrate their mastery of the process in question. But you and the training coordinator can also use the matrix to keep track of the training schedule. When training is scheduled, insert the date into the square; circle it, check it off, or block it out when training is complete.

Reinforce Training With Coaching and Immediate Opportunities to Apply the New Knowledge and Skills

Some team members will come out of training rarin' to go; others will be feeling pretty insecure. You may need to restrain the former and push the latter out of the nest. As a coach, it's your job to do both without breaking your two covenants: You will transfer the responsibility, and you won't desert your team.

To show your commitment to both these promises, meet with newly trained team members for a discussion of next steps. Good questions will inspire both the overconfident and the fearful to plot out a careful path and proceed judiciously. You might ask:

- How well did the training match your expectations and teach you what you hoped to learn?
- How will you be able to apply what you learned to _____[fill in with specific needs of the team]_____ ?
- What problems do you anticipate?
- What ideas do you have for dealing with those problems?
- What plans do you have for handling _____[fill in with other typical problems confronted in managing this process]_____ ?
- What's the first thing you would like to do?
- What will be the impact of doing that?
- How will you measure your own performance?
- What help will you need?
- What help do you want from me?

If a team member remains insecure about assuming her designated responsibilities, work side by side with her for a time, or let her serve as your assistant until she is ready to stand on her own.

Create an Atmosphere That Encourages the Application of New Knowledge and Skills

Too often, what follows training is business as usual. People practice new skills in the classroom, but back on the job they are blocked from applying them by fear of failure, looming crises, or the subtle pressure of the status quo. Here are some ways to abolish those fears:

- *Make it a norm that the team will manage itself, rather than look to management for directions.* At Northern Telecom, the developmental meetings on efficiency had an immediate payoff. One day, a team member used her new knowledge to recognize that the team's efficiency measurements for that day would be poor. But the problem, she complained to Tim Smith, had nothing to do with the team's real efficiency. It hadn't been able to get started on time because the circuit boards weren't ready.

"That's not our fault," the worker grumbled. "Somebody should do something about that."

"Who do you think should do that?" Smith responded.

As Smith tells the rest of the story, "It just hit her. She went home that night and drew up a plan. The next day she brought it to her team. With some modifications, they implemented the plan."

• *Provide resources.* Share sources of information and contacts with outsiders who are at the opposite end of a work process — vendors, customers, people in other departments.

You should also provide time — minutes or hours at meetings to discuss successes and failures and learn from both; days, weeks, or months to master old processes and try out new ones. Go to bat for the team with management or outsiders if they threaten to judge the team too quickly.

In addition, be a resource yourself — judiciously. Knowing when to give an answer and when to point the questioner in the direction of discovery is more of an art than a science. When teams were new at GE's Plant III, people would ask Cell Leader Bill Harding simple questions like "When are the parts coming from the vendor?" It would have been easy to pick up the phone and call, but Harding resisted. "That's really the responsibility of the team," he says. "In cases like that you need to say, 'Here's the telephone number. Why don't you give them a call?'"

At Titeflex, Team Manager Dave Litwin is known for telling workers, "Here's where you go to get the information." But, says Chief Steward Ralph Galarneau, "if the people don't have time to go in search of information, Dave will be a resource."

• *Treat mistakes as opportunities to learn.* Teams will make business mistakes. And there will be times when you will have to bite your tongue and sit by and watch them do it. But that's no excuse for zapping them with an "I told you so" or, even worse, "Well, I expected this to happen, but I had to let you find out for yourselves." That comment comes across as a set-up, not an expression of freedom.

What is called for are some probing questions: What went wrong? What could you have done differently? Have you thought about ____[fill in your ideas for a better approach]___? What will you do next time?

• *Anticipate and deal with obstacles.* Resistance from the employees themselves may be the first obstacle you encounter when your organization initiates self-directed work teams. For every person chomping at the bit to take over management responsibilities, there will probably be at least one other whose response is, "You're not paying me to do this."

With a union contract to uphold, Titeflex couldn't have forced teams on workers even if it had wanted to. There were a few individuals who refused to participate at first. But when the long-term employees jumped on the bandwagon quickly, others followed suit.

Smith at Northern Telecom says the majority of new team members are at least skeptical, if not outright antagonistic, at the beginning. His advice is not to push the reluctant ones and to start with those who want to learn. Eventually the others will want to get on board. "Our philosophy is: Take it when you are ready," he says.

To help people get ready, Smith advises, give them management responsibilities in incremental steps.

"Start with easier tasks," he suggests. At Northern Telecom, each team's first tasks were simply to pick a name for the team and to choose a team logo, meeting place and time, and team roles. Even agreeing on those things took time, up to several months for a few teams.

When the employees begin to coalesce as teams, you can introduce the least complex tasks of managing work processes. When its teams had reached this point, for example, Northern Telecom began having developmental meetings to teach employees to use efficiency measurements. This was a good topic to introduce at this stage because, says Smith, "you can get the concepts across very quickly."

As teams begin to develop a sense of mastery, you can move on to more complicated processes. At Northern Telecom, the next stage was teaching teams about quality. "The thrust was: How can you fix a problem long term by improving the process, rather than focusing on not making errors," Smith explains.

But team members themselves won't be the only recalcitrant individuals. You should also anticipate some early resistance from people outside the unit whose cooperation is critical to the team's success: technical experts, administrative officials, vendors, clients. Any of these may be distrustful of a new team's authority and competence. Prepare to run interference for the team until it establishes credibility and contacts of its own.

Monitor Progress

As teams assume the management of work, team coaches keep abreast of team performance in three ways: through regularly scheduled meetings of representatives of all the teams in the unit, chaired by the coach; through regular meetings of each team, chaired by the team leader but attended by the coach; and through plenty of informal contact.

At Titeflex, Team Manager Litwin meets three times a week with representatives of all thirteen aerospace manufacturing cells. He reviews metrics for each cell that highlight the status of all the major work processes on both a daily and a monthly basis. He examines the previous day's output, measured against the daily target; the current day's status, including work in process, number of jobs in the cell at the start of the day, number of jobs in subassembly and rework, and number inspected; and month-to-date numbers.

For each of three shifts, GE's Plant III holds weekly ten-minute business review meetings attended by everyone on the shop floor to review weekly and year-to-date performance. The plant manager and a group of coaches — including cell, production, maintenance, and quality leaders — also attend daily pass-on meetings prior to each shift, where cell associates (chosen on a rotating basis) get together to review what's happened in the previous eight hours. The cell associates take that information back to cell start-up meetings where the team decides who will do what that day.

At individual team meetings, the coach's job is to listen, learn, and provide support without taking over. Weed of Bell Atlantic says that she attends some, but not all, of her two teams' one-hour weekly meetings. Even when she attends, unless she has to discuss a particular agenda item, she observes without participating. Her role, she says, is to make sure that the team members stick to their own agreements about their meeting processes. For example, although the teams decide the number of people necessary for a quorum, occasionally she has to restrain them from making a decision at meetings even though they lack a quorum.

Bill Crockett of Texas Instruments asks teams to provide biweekly status reports covering what's going on, what they need, and their plans for two weeks. Every six weeks he schedules meetings with each team's star points to review action plan status against goals, plans, and problems. He also attends, but doesn't chair, regular review meetings among corresponding star points from all the teams. These meetings have turned out to be such a good place to find out what's happening that resource people and other managers attend, as well.

But, for keeping track of progress, formal meetings are only half the story. Says Crockett, "I try to communicate informally with each team daily. There's no replacement for staying in touch."

Provide Feedback and Ongoing Support

"Focus on the process, not the person," stresses Harding of GE, describing how he delivers constructive feedback. He elaborates, "When there's an issue, for example, the cost of operations, we get the whole team together and try to find out what's wrong."

Harding's feedback process offers additional lessons:

• *Stay away from the trap of blame.* "At first," he recalls, "the group would try to assign blame, saying 'It's another shift's fault.' It took a while to establish the idea that we're not here to assign blame but to find a way to refine, foolproof the process."

• *Encourage everyone's contributions without criticism or retaliation.* "These sessions are very freewheeling," Harding says. "Nobody feels threatened. We haven't taken disciplinary actions, and nobody gets stabbed in the back."

There are additional ways to provide feedback. When Crockett of Texas Instruments reviews his teams' biweekly status reports, he writes comments on them, giving encouragement or asking questions if necessary. In his shop this kind of feedback gets a wide audience, since his comments generally get posted on the bulletin boards.

Of course, giving feedback doesn't always result in the team's solving its own problem. The coach may have to get more directly involved. Advises Crockett, "Give them feedback; give all the tools to solve the problem themselves. Then if they can't, give coaching or ask someone else to come in and help." Here he uses "coaching" to mean recommending solutions. "Have you considered this?" the team coach might say to introduce a suggestion for solving the problem.

Recognize and Reward Accomplishments

Even more important than delivering constructive feedback to correct performance problems is providing positive feedback to reward accomplishments.

Litwin at Titeflex starts his thrice-weekly status meetings with praise for what the teams have done right. At one such meeting, he congratulated team members for reaching their goal for work in progress. Then he led a round of applause in response to the report he'd received after a recent visit from the president of Titeflex's parent company, Bundy Corporation. "The visitor on Tuesday said the factory looked very, very good, the nicest Bundy plant he's been in," he told meeting attendees. "Give yourself a clap."

At GE, Harding takes a no-holds-barred approach to recognizing good work. "Blow good things out of proportion" is his philosophy. He adds, "I never let anyone go home without saying thank you."

9

Solving Work Problems

When teams are new, you can expect the members to alternate between pulling you in and pushing you away when problems arise. Volunteer a suggestion and you might get your knuckles rapped. "Leave us alone," they'll remind you sharply. "We can handle this." Turn your back and they may come pounding on your door, demanding that you tell them what to do.

Particularly if you were formerly the boss of the team members, they'll remember all the times they perceived you as interfering when they were certain that their solution was better (as it may well have been if you operated in the kind of hierarchical environment that paid no heed to worker suggestions). When the going gets tough, however, they'll fall back on the old habit of looking to you for answers. In the old environment, after all, whether you were right or wrong didn't matter much to them. Their job, as the people at Titeflex say, "was to leave their brains at the door."

That's changed. The main reason is described by Vice Chairman Richard Plumley of Plumley Companies in Paris, Tennessee. "Over the past twenty years," he says, "manufacturers have recognized that workers are the best source of problem identification. The real leap is to create a situation—through education and skills training—where the best source is also the best solver."

Self-directed work teams, with members trained in problem solving, create just that situation.

The Team Coach's New Role

Just because you used to be the supervisor doesn't mean you have to have all the answers, or that you should share them if you do—at least not immediately. This is a marked change for Wanda Vinson of Bell Atlantic's Consumer Sales unit in Beltsville, Maryland. Solving customer problems is a regular part of her team's job. "Employees still come to me and ask, 'What shall I do?'" she says. "In the old environment, I'd say, 'Do this, do that.' In the self-directed environment, I stop, step back, and help the person through problem solving."

"It's tricky," she adds. Tricky, yes, because, like every team coach, she's doing a balancing act between sharing information and sharing power. Sometimes urging teams or individual team members to solve their own problems feels like wasted effort, as if you were asking them to reinvent the wheel when you've got the spokes and the rim in your desk drawer; it often seems as if it would be more efficient simply to give them an answer and send them on their way.

But in the long run, you'll save your time and theirs if at some point they no longer have to bring you all their problems. And far from asking them to reinvent the wheel, you're giving them the opportunity to replace it with jet-propelled wings.

Team problem solving pits the collective knowledge of all team members against the problems that the team confronts. "As a traditional manager, one half of your time is spent getting information from employees to make decisions," estimates Tim Smith, business unit manager at Northern Telecom. "Teams don't have to do that; among the members they already have the information." When teams solve their own problems, the result is often a better solution and more buy-in than if you had dictated the way to go.

The kind of support you need to provide will depend on the problem-solving forum. For some issues the team will meet to do formal problem solving. You may be asked to facilitate, but more often that function will be handled by

Figure 9–1.   Steps to problem solving.

1. Identify the problem.
2. Identify the causes.
3. Determine the criteria for a solution.
4. Generate options.
5. Determine the solution(s).
6. Develop implementation plans.
7. Review results regularly.

the team leader or an outside facilitator. If you are not the facilitator, your job will be a subtle one — to support the process, help keep it on track, ensure that all views are heard, encourage consensus, but discourage groupthink — all without appearing to step in and take over!

More often, you and the team will be confronted by work problems that arise unexpectedly and need spontaneous solutions. Once they become used to the process, teams will use the same methods for solving problems on the spur of the moment that they use in a formal setting — albeit in a somewhat curtailed form when urgency is the driving force.

Many times, individual team members will come to you for help in solving work problems that may not affect other team members. Even then, you and that employee can adapt the process outlined in Figure 9–1 to come to a logically derived solution. The biggest difference will be that arriving at consensus will be easy.

Identify the Problem

Often defining the problem is the hardest part. Everyone has a different take on it: "The problem is that our computers are outdated." "The problem is that our software never was adequate." "The problem is that no one knows how to use the system." The team needs to get everyone's views out into the open.

In a problem-solving meeting, keep a close watch for

team members who aren't contributing their ideas. If you are not the facilitator, you're in an excellent position to do this. When you know someone is holding back, intercede with a question like, "Pat, what were the comments you were making about this at lunch the other day? I think they were relevant."

Sometimes a particularly vocal group will dominate a session, leaving the more reserved members out in the cold. If that happens, you might follow the lead of Karen Page of Texas Instruments, who interjects what she suspects is the quiet person's point of view. She doesn't become insistent about it, but she gets it out there for discussion.

If you are working one-on-one with a team member, prod the person to look at the problem in new ways by asking questions like, "Why do you think that is happening?" "Put yourself in the customer's shoes. What do you think of the problem from that point of view?"

Identify the Causes

To get to the root problem, the team needs to dig out causes. Otherwise it risks mistaking a symptom for the real problem, which will lead eventually to a recurrence of the situation. Whether you are an observer at a team meeting or a coach in a one-on-one session, keep asking, "What do you think is causing that?" and "Why?" "Why?" "Why?"

The answers to those questions may not be in the room. Encourage employees to seek information from other teams, technical departments, vendors, customers — whoever may have the answers — before considering any solutions.

Employees at GE's Plant III use a process called fluorescent penetrant inspection (FPI) to identify tiny defects in engineered aircraft parts. FPI revealed an ongoing problem with a series of parts, requiring increased rework. At a problem-solving meeting, the team's first take on the cause was to place blame, charging a coworker on the night shift with benching a bunch of bad parts. In that meeting there was no way that the team could answer the next question: Why

did the worker's parts turn out bad? It took more investiga-
tion to reveal that the worker accused of benching bad parts
had been issued a set of tools with burrs on them. The
problem was not an unskilled or uncaring worker. It was
bad tools.

Determine the Criteria for a Solution

Even when they've established the underlying causes of the
problem, encourage team members to go through one
more step before seeking a solution. Ask them to define the
criteria for the solution they'll choose: What results do they
want? For example, they may decide that any new computer
system must process reports in three formats, compiling information fed in as raw data from twelve locations. What
results do they definitely not want? Perhaps the cost must
not exceed $100,000. Rank ordering or voting usually helps
teams determine what criteria are most important from
those suggested.

Encouraging the team members to focus on desired
results helps them to consider a wide range of possible
approaches to accomplishing those results. Keep team
members from fixating on what is wrong, which inevitably
leads more to blame-fixing than to solutions, and discourage them at this stage from concentrating on what they
think they need, which can restrict their thinking. If they decide they need a new computer system, that is a solution,
not a problem, and it limits them to just one way of solving
the real problem.

Generate Options

The more possibilities the team can generate, the better its
chances of discovering a superior solution. The most popular method of generating possible solutions is brainstorming, a fast-paced, freewheeling session in which team
members blurt out any and every idea that comes to mind.
All ideas from the logical to the ludicrous are recorded with-

out assessment. In most groups, brainstorming unearths a wealth of ideas.

To get the most out of brainstorming:

- *Enforce the no-criticism, no-judging rule.* The surest way to kill a brainstorming session is to criticize an idea as it is offered. Who would risk offering the next suggestion?
- *Encourage brainstormers to think outside their usual framework.* Ask questions like, "What if size (or time, space, materials, format) didn't matter?" or "What if we could do it backwards?" Sometimes the wildest suggestion triggers a line of thinking that leads to an innovative solution.
- *Encourage everyone to participate.* Ask a silent team member, "Chris, what would make the last suggestion work better for you?"
- *Ask team members what other people have done to solve similar problems.* It makes sense to borrow all the ideas you can and adapt them to your own situation.

Determine the Solution(s)

Even after the team's list of possible solutions is complete, it is too early to jump directly to choosing the best one (or best ones — since you may have more than one cause, you may need more than one solution). Premature choices will be based at best on people's intuition or, at worst, on their prejudices.

To make better choices, the team needs to judge each alternative solution against the list of criteria or desired results. You or the facilitator can make a matrix with criteria running across the top and the alternatives listed down the side. Team members can rate each alternative on a scale from 1 to 5 and then total the score for each option.

The team can also evaluate alternatives by listing the pluses and minuses of each. Do the negatives of some alternatives outweigh the potential benefits? Can the minuses be overcome by changing the suggestion a little?

Sometimes a clear best solution emerges in the evaluation activity. Just as likely, some alternatives will drop right out of consideration, a bunch will appear unlikely, and a few will have strong possibilities. If you are working with an individual, encourage the person to reassess the criteria and reevaluate until the best solutions emerge.

Solution by Consensus

If it's a team problem, here's where consensus building comes in. Consensus decision making doesn't mean that everyone has to love the accepted decision. The decision doesn't even have to be everyone's first choice. Consensus decision making does require that all team members feel able to live with the decision and be willing to commit to fulfilling their roles in its implementation.

Although finding one solution that everyone can live with isn't easy and seldom happens quickly, ultimately it's worth the effort because the buy-in by the group is so much greater than when a solution is imposed or arrived at by majority vote. When majority rules, what often really happens is that the minority quietly undermines the decision made.

Even when a group is committed to making decisions by consensus, you can suggest that the team take a straw vote now and then to reveal where the group stands. You may discover that everyone likes one or two ideas best, simplifying your task. Or you may find that there are some ideas that no one is committed to and that can be dropped from consideration.

If you are the facilitator and you get a sense that everyone is leaning in one direction, ask, "Is there anyone who can't live with this?" If some individuals raise objections, ask, "What modifications would make it acceptable?" Or pick the two or three most favored alternatives, and ask for suggestions for combining them. Some techniques for helping the team reach consensus are listed in Figure 9–2.

Keep seeking agreement, but be sure to draw out any reservations and air them. Otherwise, the solution may fall

Figure 9–2.   Consensus-building tools.

* *Straw votes*—to limit the option to a manageable number
* *Making modifications*—to win over a holdout
* *Creating combinations*—when two or three choices are better than one
* *Airing reservations*—to avoid groupthink or passive resistance
* *Reassessing and re-evaluating*—to get a fresh start
* *Taking a break*—when progress bogs down
* *Having trial runs*—to lessen the fear of making a mistake

victim to groupthink, resulting in a mediocre outcome that no one wants to criticize or an outrageous idea that's way off mark.

Achieving consensus can be hard work and take a lot of time. If you sense that the group is getting discouraged, call a break of fifteen minutes, a day, or a week. Then have the group reassess the criteria and re-evaluate the alternatives. Sometimes a break leads to breakthrough thinking.

If fear of making a mistake keeps the group from deciding anything, remind team members that no decision is cast in stone. Try Karen Page's approach: "You may say, 'Let's do it for a week. Maybe three days. We reserve the right to say we were stupid and change our mind. Go with this and we'll revisit in a week.'" Don't impose a decision, but don't let the group get so bogged down in problem solving that it never gets around to putting a solution into action.

Develop Implementation Plans

Encourage the team to name a champion to take overall responsibility for the implementation of the solution. Break the solution into steps, and assign each step to the best person for the task. Determine outputs, deliverables, and deadlines.

Review Results Regularly

If the implementation plan includes achievement milestones, the team can match its actual results against those milestones and determine if any changes in the plan are necessary. You'll need to keep an overview of what's happening, but encourage the team to monitor itself.

When new problems arise during implementation—and what plan ever got carried through without a hitch?—chances are you'll find yourself back in a balancing act. Do you give answers or throw the questions back at the team? Making that choice is part of the art of team coaching.

10

Running a Business

Patty Barten, vice president of Motorola's Cellular Products Division, enjoys talking about her team-based operation in human terms, stressing how people like to work there and describing the emphasis on educational opportunities and career growth. Then, just in case the listener starts to wonder if all of this soft stuff comes at the expense of good business, Barten makes it very clear: "I want to emphasize that this is not just fluff or fairy dust. We always get back to bottom-line results. We operate each work cell as a business."

At GE's Plant III, Plant Manager Jerry Labadini puts it in dollar terms. "We try to make the cells autonomous," he says. "Each is a $3 to $4 million business."

For most nonmanagement employees, running a $3 to $4 million business involves learning a new set of tasks and requires a new set of skills. It's up to the team coach to see that team members understand the tasks, have the skills, and run their business to support the objectives of the organization.

If you are a team coach, one of your responsibilities is to guide team members through the basic business functions of setting goals, creating and implementing action plans, and developing and managing a budget.

Setting Team Goals

In every organization, some goals are determined at a management level and handed to the teams. Often teams are

Figure 10–1. Characteristics of good team goals.

* Contribute to organizational objectives
* Respond to customer needs
* Reflect team's key responsibilities
* Contain measurable standards
* Generate doable action plans

invited to have input into these goals, but the ultimate decision rests with upper management. But this reality doesn't restrict teams from setting additional goals of their own. In fact, most organizations encourage them to do so, and some require it. Figure 10–1 contains a list of the qualities common to good team goals.

As a team coach, your role in the goal-setting process can vary. Unless team members can enroll in a good goal-setting workshop provided by your training department or an outside vendor, you may need to provide training. Unless your company can provide an organization development specialist or your team leader is ready to take on the task, you'll probably be called upon to facilitate the goal-setting process. At the very least, even if your team is advanced, you'll need to review the goals and monitor the team's progress as it pursues them.

If you guide the process from the beginning, you'll need to:

1. *Obtain copies of the organization's mission, priorities, and annual business plan and your business unit or department plan, and distribute them to team members.* Good team goals aren't written in a vacuum. They need to support organizational objectives. For that to happen, teams need all the information you can provide about the plans, strategies, and key initiatives of upper management. Bill Crockett of Texas Instruments says, "One thing that helped us get the Baldrige Award was the flow down of vision regarding customer satisfaction and priorities."

At GE's Plant III, the management team developed goals for areas such as quality, cost, and manufacturing losses, and then taught them to all employees at a six-week training program that preceded the reopening of the plant as a team-based operation. Based on those goals, the first group of trainees actually wrote the plant's mission statement, calling for the plant to be the lowest-cost, highest-quality, on-time-delivery engine manufacturing company in the world. When individual teams write their goals, they know it's their own mission that's behind them.

2. *Help teams determine opportunities and constraints created by the mission, priorities, and plan.* If the organization's focus is on cost cutting, for example, the team may use the opportunity to implement team members' innovations using existing equipment, but such a focus will forestall any hopes of achieving a goal that requires a major investment in capital equipment. In a similar vein, as Michelle Thomas, production manager at Motorola, points out, it makes no sense to focus on improving the production of a product that the company is going to phase out anyway.

3. *Help team members determine the customers' needs.* Give team members access to information you have, or can get, about customers. Introduce them to customers so that they can gather information on their own. Arrange for visits to customers so that team members can see for themselves how their product or service is being used. Without their visit to a GE plant, Titeflex workers would not have understood that they weren't meeting GE's requirements at that time.

4. *Encourage teams to pinpoint their key responsibilities and describe how they contribute to fulfilling the organization's objectives and customer needs.* Ask the whole team these questions:

— Why does the team exist?
— What are the critical products, services, or results without which there would be no reason for the team to exist?
— What contributions can the team make that will have an impact on the business plan?

At first glance the answers to the first two questions may seem obvious, but you and the team members will probably be surprised at the variety of responses different members will provide. When they've come to consensus on their key responsibilities, team members will be ready to identify the contributions the organization needs most from them.

5. *For each key responsibility, have the team determine the desired outputs.* Company priorities usually determine desired outputs. For example, if a team's key responsibility is to produce computer chips, then, depending upon the company's priorities, the desired outputs might stress high productivity, improved quality, excellent safety record, and consistent on-time deliveries.

6. *Help the team establish standards for measuring the desired outputs and express each output as a measurable goal.* What is high productivity or excellent service? Does your productivity measurement simply count the number of widgets per person per hour, or does it factor in the many other things people do besides build widgets? Is the quality of service determined by the absence of complaints, the number of compliments, or the way complaints are handled? These questions don't always have a right answer, but your team can come to a consensus on the members' definition, expressed as a precise measurement that allows no room for interpretation so that there's no argument later about when or whether the goal was met.

7. *Assist each team in prioritizing its goals.* After they've been through steps one to six, teams may have more goals than they can realistically work on at one time. Have each team pare its list to about three, by analyzing each goal in terms of its contribution to the organization's objectives, its potential for improving customer satisfaction, and its importance relative to the team's other goals.

Developing Action Plans

Planning their own work is one of the first management functions teams are asked to assume, sometimes even before they begin to establish their own goals. At Bell Atlantic's Consumer Sales unit in Virginia Beach, the team's objectives are, for the most part, set by the organization, says team developer Krissan Zoby. But teams have developed action plans for several areas of responsibility, including service, collection, and culture change. Their plans, which are different for each team, include ways to monitor their progress.

"They did their plans on their own," Zoby says, "with some, but not a lot, of direction from us." Providing "direction" meant pointing out to one team that its plan for conducting three studies at one time could be overwhelming and explaining to another team that certain times of the year were better than others for some activities. Her suggestions kept teams from making major mistakes, pointed them toward opportunities, and improved their planning processes.

Creating action plans is likely to be a new activity for team members. In Zoby's unit, for example, the old way was for the assistant managers to go off-site for a day or two and come back with action plans for the groups.

As a team coach, you may be called upon to facilitate a team planning session or to support such a session facilitated by the team leader. You will help the team if you:

• *Keep team members focused on the goal that the plan addresses and the standards by which success will be measured.* It's tempting to bring a lot of separate agendas to a planning session and to try to work them all in, much like legislators attach their favorite riders to unrelated bills. When planners get off target or bog down in minutiae, draw their attention back to the goal to get them back on track.

• *Suggest they assign one individual the overseer's responsibility.* This person's job is to ensure that no important tasks fall through the cracks, that actions don't get wastefully duplicated, and that the plan is implemented according to schedule. But make sure the team doesn't dump the plan on one person and leave it to him or her to carry it out solo.

• *Help them develop and schedule detailed action steps.* Each action step needs a definable output, a starting date and a due date, and a person designated to carry it out. To ensure that planners don't skip or minimize steps, make sure they identify all the tasks to be done (like a giant to-do list), sequence the tasks so that they know which can be done concurrently and which are dependent upon the one preceding, estimate how long each task will take, and schedule the tasks accordingly.

• *Keep them aware of the financial impact of what they plan.* You don't have to become the money cop who keeps reminding them, "You don't have a budget for that." Instead, encourage them to monitor their own costs and revenues with questions like, "How will you accomplish that within the budget?"

• *Help them coordinate with one another, other teams, other departments, and other organizations.* In any action plan, one step, to be performed by one person, is dependent upon another step, performed by someone else. To carry out some of the tasks, team members will probably need input or cooperation from people outside the team. Make sure coordination requirements are written into the plan, and help the team make the contacts it needs to complete each step.

Developing and Managing a Budget

Self-directed work teams that are managing multimillion-dollar businesses have to make some very sophisticated financial decisions. Even teams whose financial stake is lower have to know the impact of the costs they incur and the revenue their product or service produces, directly or indirectly.

Prepare your teams to take over developing and managing their own budgets by educating them about:

• *The bottom line* — the budget total for the year.
• *Budget components* — e.g., salaries, rent, taxes, benefits,

telephone, temporary workers' and consultants' fees; depreciation of equipment; software, supplies, travel; general expenses such as books, subscriptions, and business meals. Also, business-specific items (for a publishing operation, for example, these include printing, postage, and paper).
* *Corporate, departmental, and team priorities.*
* *Functional requirements* — the needs of each function the team performs. (One person who prepares the annual budget for a large corporate department says hcr best asset is that she has had almost every job in the department.)
* *Getting help* — whom to contact for information and assistance.

Coach them so that they have the skills to:

* *Use your company's budgeting system* — complete forms accurately, and in general meet all corporate requirements.
* *Track a particular expense* — e.g., determine when a check went out to a vendor.
* *Break the annual budget down on a monthly basis and track it month to month.* This includes being able to explain variances and project actual year-end results.
* *Monitor internal charges for accuracy* (e.g., the audio/video department charges your team's budget for making twenty copies of a videotape).
* *Make workable recommendations for budget cuts or increases when necessary,* on the basis of corporate, departmental, and team priorities as well as current experience.
* *Prepare reports.* These might include personnel budget reports (e.g., costs of salaries, benefits, taxes, each person's telephone, and office or plant square footage); product cost breakdowns describing all expenses related to a product, service, or project; and vendor reports, tracking payments to specific vendors.

Be a resource to the teams. Offer:

* Insights into the process
* Contacts throughout the organization and among customers and vendors who can provide the teams with the information they need
* To go to bat for them when they need a heavy hitter to get the money they need for a cause they've justified to your satisfaction

Part IV

Guiding a Team to Self-Manage Its Members

One of the biggest challenges that faces self-directed work teams is managing the performance of the team members. Not only are new team members likely to be unfamiliar with the fine points of personnel policies; they are almost always uncomfortable passing judgment on the work of their peers, confronting their friends' performance shortfalls, or even singling out individuals for special recognition.

If you are a former supervisor, you may continue to perform some of these management functions while new teams get their bearings and build their confidence and know-how and until the organization trusts the teams to take on such responsibilities. But your goal is to prepare the teams to assume these functions themselves. The chapters in this section will help you do that.

11

Hiring Employees and Appraising Their Performance

How much influence do self-directed work teams have in hiring new employees and evaluating team members' performance? Across a selection of team-based organizations, the answers to these questions range from almost none to almost total. But one answer does fit them all: The team's influence in these functions is growing.

Who Hires?

In Bell Atlantic's Consumer Sales office in Virginia Beach, the human resources department does the hiring, reports Krissan Zoby. But teams can determine the new hiree's job placement. In one case, when a collection center team lost its credit bureau person, HR brought in an employee from another office with extensive credit bureau experience. Instead of giving the new person the credit bureau job, however, the team decided that what it really needed was more help in active collections, where team members deal with customers with working telephone service. So the team decided to train the new person in active collections and operate without a dedicated credit person, sharing that role among them all.

At Texas Instruments' McKinney Board Shop, team members have a say in whom the plant brings in as contract workers. (The plant was not hiring permanent workers as this book was being researched.) Karen Page reports that a mixed team of facilitators and workers interviews prospects. Before the interviews, the workers develop a list of questions to help them decide if they want each interviewee.

At the far end of the spectrum is Titeflex, where teams not only hire their own people but have input into who gets hired by the company into technical support jobs, such as engineers. After prescreening by management, technical job candidates meet with team members. The final selection is arrived at by consensus between team members and management.

Prepare Teams to Interview

Even if screening job candidates is still your responsibility, encourage teams to take an active part. You can help teams prepare for the challenge of selecting the best job candidates by arranging for them to get training in how to interview or by educating them yourself in the legal dos and don'ts and in the best practices for conducting employment interviews.

Make sure team members know that they should avoid asking any questions about race, national origin, or religion; marital and family status; age or date of birth; arrest and conviction records; credit rating; friends or relatives who work for the company; or appearance.[1] Furthermore, before bringing up any discussion of education, physical or experience requirements, or availability for Saturday or Sunday work, interviewers need to determine what the bona fide job requirements are.

Determine Job Requirements

When a specific job opening arises, work with the team to define the skills and characteristics to look for in candidates.

1. *Affirmative Action and Equal Employment: A Guide for Employers* (Washington, D.C., 1974).

More than anyone else, team members know the precise job skills required, especially if they've been conducting cross-training. They can also provide a list of the personal characteristics that would contribute to successful job performance. If they are novices at this task, you may have to help them distinguish bona fide job requirements from qualities that are merely desirable. If a warehouse team defines the ideal candidate as a "strong young man," for example, the team coach's task is to guide the team to the realization that what the job really requires is someone who can move heavy boxes using equipment that is available (or, within the guidelines of the Americans with Disabilities Act, equipment that can be obtained without undue hardship to the organization).

Trust Team Members' Judgment

When it comes to making a choice among candidates, trust the judgment of the team members. They know that the performance of the new person will have a big impact on the success of their team, and they'll choose the person whose impact will be the most positive. Titeflex Operations Manager Kevin Roberts admits that workers have convinced him to change his mind about whom to hire for a technical support job. In hindsight, he's convinced the workers were right.

Peer Appraisals

Most team-based organizations employ some form of peer review in their performance appraisal systems. If they don't, the reason is as likely to be union opposition as management resistance. Some organizations don't conduct formal performance reviews at all because of union opposition.

More commonly, team members fill out rating forms on their peers and submit them to a manager who compiles the submissions, adds his or her own, combines them into a rating, and holds a review meeting with each employee. In a few organizations, the teams themselves conduct the review meetings, led by trained worker/facilitators.

After struggling with peer appraisal systems that either unduly rewarded the most popular team members or gave mushy middle-to-good ratings to everyone, Tim Smith of Northern Telecom's Nashville Repair and Distribution Center devised a rating form that, he says, solves both those problems. (Smith's report on the system and a sample form are reproduced in Figures 11–1 and 11–2.) Each team member gets a copy of a form, which includes five performance categories: productivity, quality, teamwork, customer orientation, and safety/housekeeping; categories are defined on a separate sheet. Under each category heading, workers are instructed to list the names of exactly one half of the members of their team—the top half, those who best fulfill the category requirements enumerated in the definition.

The manager rates each employee on a four-point scale in each category, and then collects the peer forms, tallies the votes, and converts them into quartile scores. Using established formulae that allow no managerial discretion, the manager then combines the peer scores with his or her own ratings to determine category and overall ratings for each employee. (See Figures 11–3 and 11–4.) These ratings form the basis for a performance review meeting between the manager and each employee.

At Motorola, team members also fill out evaluation forms on their teammates. On the forms, they rate the employee on seven criteria. The supervisor compiles all team member evaluations into a composite and translates the results into scores. However, says Vice President Patty Barten, the organization is in the process of moving away from scores completely.

Whether performance appraisal meetings are conducted by team members, by you as coach, or by your manager, you need to understand the system and prepare team members for their role in it. Help them understand that:

Figure 11–1. NRDC peer evaluation.

WHO:

All production, maintenance, and materials employees

WHEN:

The last month of each quarter

WHY:

Managers often away from work areas
Promotes team development/empowerment
More fair to employees
Gives authority to go with responsibility

DEVELOPMENT:

Lots of research—articles, other companies, consultants
Tried several types of programs
Several "practice runs" before implementation

HOW IT WORKS:

Form lists five major performance categories
Category definitions on a separate sheet
Manager gives form to each team member
Member votes for "top half" in each category
Member completes in private—can take home
Member folds sheet, manager picks up

RESULTS:

Manager tallies votes for each member, each category
Manager uses sheet (attached) to determine quartile scores
Quartile scores listed on employee's Performance Review Sheet
Member's final rating in each category is determined
Manager reviews Performance Review with employee
Members see only their own scores, not others' scores

FEATURES:

Good differentiation—trials with each member rating each other member on a 1–5 scale proved worthless, because all members averaged 3.5–4.5 in every category
Members can't give best friend highest ratings or "lowball" anyone they don't like
Forced ranking keeps team from giving everyone the same raise

Source: Internal communication of Northern Telecom's Nashville Repair and Distribution Center. Used with permission.

Figure 11–2. Peer evaluation form.

Please Vote for the Top 5 in Each Category (Only 5)

Employee	Productivity	Quality	Teamwork	Customer Orientation	Safety & House- keeping
Name 1	_____	_____	_____	_____	_____
Name 2	_____	_____	_____	_____	_____
Name 3	_____	_____	_____	_____	_____
Name 4	_____	_____	_____	_____	_____
Name 5	_____	_____	_____	_____	_____
Name 6	_____	_____	_____	_____	_____
Name 7	_____	_____	_____	_____	_____
Name 8	_____	_____	_____	_____	_____
Name 9	_____	_____	_____	_____	_____
Name 10	_____	_____	_____	_____	_____

Source: Tim Smith, business unit manager, Northern Telecom. Used with permission.

Figure 11–3. Ranking as a percentage of highest score.

If the Highest Score Is:	0–25%	26–50%	51–75%	76–100%
2	0	1		2
3	0	1	2	3
4	1	2	3	4
5	1	2	3	4, 5
6	1	2, 3	4	5, 6
7	1	2, 3	4, 5	6, 7
8	1, 2	3, 4	5, 6	7, 8
9	1, 2	3, 4	5, 6	7, 8, 9
10	1, 2	3, 4, 5	6, 7	8, 9, 10

Example: Assume that in the productivity category on the Peer Evaluation Form, the highest number of votes awarded any team member was 9. Then a team member who received 5 votes would fall into the third quartile, 51–75%.

Source: Tim Smith, business unit manager, Northern Telecom. Used with permission.

Figure 11–4. Chart to determine overall score (for each category).

Peer	Manager	Overall
0–25 %	NI	NI
0–25	A	A
0–25	E	A
26–50	NI	NI
26–50	A	A
26–50	E	A
51–75	NI	A
51–75	A	A
51–75	E	E
76–100	NI	A
76–100	A	A
76–100	E	E

E = Exceeded Expectations
A = Achieved Expectations
NI = Needs Improvement
*UP = Unsatisfactory Performance
*NOTE Can be used only if there is documented disciplinary action in the employee file.

Source: Tim Smith, business unit manager, Northern Telecom. Used with permission.

- Appraisals are not popularity contests. Appraisals are assessments of skills, not evidence of friendship.
- Appraisal forms are not scorecards. Their purpose is to identify where people excel so that those skills can be put to best use and where people need to improve so that they can get the training and coaching that will help them perform better—to the benefit of the whole team.
- Rating everyone about the same (if the system allows it) is a cop-out that waters down the system, making it meaningless.
- The purpose of appraisal meetings is not to judge each other but to provide specific, objective, positive

and negative feedback on performance as team members have observed and measured it. (For more on feedback, see Chapter 13.)

- Feedback on interpersonal behaviors is appropriate to the extent that those behaviors affect the performance of the team.

12

Recognizing and Rewarding Accomplishments

Implementing self-directed work teams inevitably changes the way organizations recognize and reward their employees. Traditional reward systems, which encourage individual achievement, can actually conflict with the goals and structure of teams.

Teams rely on cooperation. That's why, when her top production workers gloated about beating someone else's record, Motorola's Joan Clarke challenged them to help others on the team top their new record.

A reward system based on ranking employees or recognizing a few award winners can, at worst, encourage people to hoard information, undercut their fellow workers, and resist helping each other. Some experts therefore recommend eliminating individual incentives in team-based organizations entirely and replacing them with team rewards. The other side to that argument is that rewarding all team members identically, whether they are high or low contributors, is likely to cause resentment among the top performers and give the slackers no incentive to improve.

At the institutional level, some organizations with mature teams resolve the dilemma by instituting a two-tiered reward system that provides team rewards for meeting team goals and individual rewards based on peer evaluations. For the team coach, an excellent approach to recognizing and rewarding individuals and teams is summed up in Clarke's approach: "Acknowledge when people do well," she advises, "but reward the whole group for a complete effort."

Be sure to recognize teams when they:

- Accomplish annual, monthly, or weekly goals
- Reach milestones on their way to goal accomplishment
- Innovate with a new work process
- Do something special for a customer
- Acquire a new customer
- Cut costs
- Increase revenue
- Help another team
- Overcome an obstacle
- Solve a big problem or a smaller irritant
- Demonstrate exceptional teamwork
- Achieve a new level if your organization has a structured development plan for teams
- Take on extra work

You don't need a big budget—which you almost certainly won't have—to reward teams in a meaningful way. Be creative about coming up with rewards that money can't buy. Here are some suggestions to get you started:

- Arrange for a thank-you visit or phone call from the company president.
- Arrange for thank-you letters from the company president to be sent to every team member.
- Send thank-you letters yourself.
- Send letters to the team members' families, expressing your appreciation for the work the team has done, explaining specifically what the team accomplished and what it means to you and the company. This is especially appropriate if the team has been putting in a lot of overtime.
- Arrange to have an article about the team's accomplishment published in the organization's newsletter.

- If your team provides a service for the rest of the organization, write an "ad" for the newsletter, touting the team, the people in it, and the service it provides.
- Arrange for the team to make a presentation on its accomplishment to the top brass.

Think twice before offering any reward that pits one team against another, such as an award for the team with the highest productivity. It's true that some people are turned on by competition, but there is a dangerous downside. For every winner, there are a number of losers who may have worked very hard and yet get no recognition. What they learn is that good work often doesn't get rewarded.

Focus instead on rewards for meeting previously established goals. Help each team set goals that are appropriate for it, and reward each team when it achieves them.

Be generous, too, with spontaneous recognition. Be very specific about the accomplishment or behavior you are acknowledging and why it's important — what it means to the company and to you personally. You might, for example, send a quick E-mail note to all team members: "I see you have topped your previous best efficiency rating. Your efforts contribute enormously toward making us the most competitive company in our field. I made a promise to the management council, and you've fulfilled it!"

Finally, you don't need to mark every worthy accomplishment with an oak leaf-inscribed plaque or a champagne celebration. Often the simplest form of recognition — a heartfelt "Thank you" — is the most meaningful.

Recognizing Individuals

A sincere thank you for a specified accomplishment or behavior is an appropriate way for a team coach to acknowledge an individual. You can also use most of the items on the list in the previous section for someone who has made an individual contribution. But for members' contributions to their teams, the most motivating recognition may come from the team itself.

Since most people feel unappreciated on their jobs, you'd think that when they got the power to recognize and reward one another, they'd use that power abundantly. But often that does not happen. Having been brought up in a business world that is stingy with its praise, members of self-directed work teams can be as miserly with their commendations as traditional managers ever were.

Situations often occur like that in Wanda Vinson's Consumer Sales unit at Bell Atlantic, where her team's designated recognition leader protested, "I'm not a recognizer," prompting a concentrated effort on Vinson's part to remind the recognition leader each time a team member does something worth acknowledging.

Vinson gives an example of the kind of performance she's striving to get the recognition leader to notice and acknowledge: "We had a period of really bad orders coming through," she recalls. The unit's computer system kicked out errors, which had to be fixed manually. One person had responsibility for correcting all the errors, and the volume of work was overwhelming. Customers didn't get billed; teams couldn't get revenue. But the person worked diligently until finally, one day, she could point to the pile of errors and say, "Look, Wanda, how thin this is."

"It's the recognizer's job," maintains Vinson, "to stay on top of performance like this."

Of course, teams aren't always niggardly in their recognition of peers. Also at Bell Atlantic, Wilma Weed says her team members write thank-you notes to each other. When one member collected $100,000 on a bad account, the team acknowledged her success with a mini-celebration. They've even recognized Weed. As she describes it, "One day I came in and there were 'We appreciate you' posters all over my office, along with a bouquet of roses and a beautiful card." The workers took her to lunch and clarified what the fanfare was all about. "They told me they appreciated my trusting them to get work done, not hovering over them," she explains.

The one reward many SDWTs don't have discretion over is money. In several of the companies highlighted in this book, monetary rewards are spelled out in and set by union contracts. In nonunion companies, management still controls the purse strings, but, increasingly, managers make their decisions based largely on team input.

Even without the power to give raises and bonuses, there are plenty of ways teams can use rewards and recognition to acknowledge and encourage good performance by team members. If you are a team coach, you can help them develop recognition systems and get accustomed to using spontaneous recognition to reinforce a job well done.

Assist teams in developing reward systems that motivate team members to perform to the peak of their ability in pursuit of team goals. Such a system must:

• *Have clearly defined reward criteria.* If a team decides to honor a "team member of the month," make sure the choice isn't based on a popularity contest. The team needs to determine in advance and publicize the precise behaviors and accomplishments that the award will recognize.

• *Give everyone an equal opportunity to earn recognition.* An award criteria based on production numbers will fail this test if some production lines are by nature faster than others. To meet this standard, the best kind of recognition is one that challenges team members to better their own records, not someone else's. For example, a team can honor all members who meet previously defined individual goals each month. Instead of posting one employee picture, the team can decorate a wall with many photos.

• *Encourage cooperation.* Suggest that a team create a special award for individuals who help others. This kind of award finds its way into the possession of quiet people who tend to stay in the background but are always there when you need them.

• *Recognize behaviors as well as outcomes.* To illustrate the difference: treating irate customers with courtesy and respect is behavior. When a dissatisfied customer decides to give your company one more chance, that's an outcome. Most rewards are for significant outcomes. That's appropriate in our bottom-line-oriented culture. But recognizing specific, desired behaviors is a way to motivate people to improve their skills, work habits, and processes and to clarify for them what behaviors the team values.

Encourage teams to recognize team members for such behaviors as cross-training a teammate (or someone from another team), mediating a conflict, volunteering to do unpleasant but necessary tasks, giving a customer extra attention, sharing information, and even making people laugh in stressful situations.

• *Build team members' self-esteem.* When people's best efforts go unrecognized and unappreciated, not only do they believe others think negatively of them; they often begin to buy into that attitude themselves. Within a team, there should be plenty of appreciation to go around. Suggest that the team find ways to recognize everyone, such as a team appreciation meeting, where every member thanks every other member for one specific helpful act.

As teams mature and as team members work together over time, learn to depend on each other, and develop trust in one another, you can expect them to recognize one another more often, spontaneously and enthusiastically. These days, when Bill Crockett of Texas Instruments makes his rounds among the workers, they'll greet him with, "Did you hear what So-and-so did?" Says Crockett, "That's a cue for me to go over and give the person a pat on the back."

13

Handling Performance Problems

Just one person whose work is not up to standard can drag down a team's performance, hold back its team development, and wreak havoc with its morale. In most teams, therefore, there is a lot of peer pressure for all members to pull their weight. When that pressure alone is not enough to keep a team member's performance from slipping, the team may go through agony before the problem is solved.

In dealing with such a situation, teams often shine if the problem is clearly a lack of job skills. They pitch in and help, coach an unskilled person on the job, and even develop job aids to guide a teammate through unfamiliar tasks.

Where they often back off is if they can see that the person can do the job but, for whatever reason, chooses not to.

"That's where they'd like to abdicate," admits Karen Page of Texas Instruments. "They'd rather come in and tell me, 'Suzy ain't doin' it,' and have me read Suzy the riot act."

Bad-Guy Syndrome

It would make sense, one might think, for those with designated team roles to handle related performance problems. Shouldn't the team's quality leader deal with a person who is making too many mistakes? Shouldn't the administrative leader confront a team member who is absent too often?

And isn't it the team leader's responsibility to work with a member whose interpersonal behavior is disruptive?

In real life these situations are likely to cause the beleaguered team role designee to object, "I'm not getting any more money for this, and you're trying to make me be the bad guy."

It's only natural that team members are very conscious of the fact that they have to work side by side with the problem person. It's going to be a pretty uncomfortable workplace if that person gets angry at them. There's even the possibility that the rest of the team will side with the accused person, blaming the confronter for raising the team's tension level.

If self-directed work teams are new in your organization, you'll probably still have the traditional supervisor's responsibility for dealing with poor performers. You can do that with the best chance of success if you follow these guidelines:

1. Before you confront the poor performer, analyze the situation, looking for situational reasons for the person's unacceptable performance. You may discover your organization's equivalent of tools with burrs on them. (Remember the GE example in Chapter 9?)

2. When you do need to counsel an employee, begin by describing the expected performance and the person's actual performance in specific, nonjudgmental terms. For example: "I expect operators on your line to produce eighty widgets a day. For the past month your average has been forty-five."

Your goal is to get the employee's cooperation in solving the problem, so don't put the person on the defensive with a vague accusation like, "Your work has been very poor lately."

3. Ask the employee what is causing the variance between expected and actual performance. You may learn something you didn't know—from bad tools to a personal problem. Or you may get defensive excuses. If that happens,

acknowledge what you heard by quickly paraphrasing and moving on without agreeing or disagreeing.

4. Describe the impact of the variance between expected and actual performance—its effect on the team, on you, and on the organization. You might say, "A shortfall of thirty-five widgets per day is going to keep your team from meeting its goals this quarter. If that happens, you and all your teammates will risk losing their bonuses. I have a stake in this, too, because I have to explain it to upper management. And the company could lose this client if we don't meet our promised quota."

What sometimes works even better is to ask the employee to describe the impact of the variance. It can be effective to force a person to confront what he or she really already knows.

5. Restate the expected performance, and ask the employee what he or she can do to correct the performance shortfall.

6. If you are satisfied with the employee's response, express confidence that the person will perform as expected. If you need to, probe for more improvement suggestions from the person, and add some of your own.

7. Come to an agreement on what the person's actions will be and what improvements are expected (in measurable terms).

8. Set a date and time for a follow-up meeting.

Team Meetings With Problem Members

In a traditional work unit, a counseling session like the one just outlined would be private, between the supervisor and the employee. One big difference in a team-based environment is that often it is appropriate for the whole team to be present. If that sounds rough, remember that your job is to train the team to take over this task. When Pete Keller of Texas Instruments facilitates such a meeting, he defines the performance problem and the team members describe the impact on the team and contribute suggestions for solving the problem. Handling the session in this fashion helps the poor performer understand the consequences of his or her actions, Keller says.

But before you risk turning a counseling session into a shouting match, make sure team members understand:

- That it's okay to confront a colleague and that it's possible to do so without stripping the person of his or her self-respect and dignity
- How to give specific, objective feedback that is descriptive, not accusatory
- How to listen objectively to someone else's point of view, and how to present their own views noncombatively
- How to paraphrase—the skill that clarifies what's been said, dispels misunderstandings, shows respect, and proves you've been listening

Pulling Out of the Process

Eventually, as the team matures, the team coach needs to draw back and encourage team members to take on the full responsibility for confronting a team member who is letting them down. When that time comes, the team coach's challenge is to get team members to realize that confrontation may be uncomfortable but that their discomfort will be even greater if they do nothing.

When an employee complains to her about "Suzy's" behavior, instead of reading Suzy the riot act, Page of Texas Instruments is likely to ask the complainer: "Why am I the right person to do this? I didn't see this happen. You did."

Then, if the complainer protests that he has to work with Suzy every day and doesn't want to get her mad at him, Page responds, "Yes, you have to work with her on a day-to-day basis, and you're the person being abused by her."

Sometimes, Page notes, there are subtle, nonconfrontational ways for a team to deal with a performance problem. She gives an example: "If someone is taking too much time off, the administrative star point can just ask, 'Is there any way you can make up this time?'" The first approach doesn't have to be an accusatory one.

When the subtle approach doesn't work, team members need to be able to take more direct action. Suffering from the impact of a team member who wasn't performing up to par, one of the teams in Page's shop not only addressed the problem with the person at a team meeting but established a performance improvement plan. The team set hourly and daily production goals for the person.

"It was hard on the person," Page concedes, "but the person's performance has improved." And the experience had another effect. "It actually made a couple of others who were borderline snap to," Page reports.

Talking *to* Versus Talking *About*

The worst thing a team can do, stresses Zoby of Bell Atlantic, is to fall into what she calls "aboutism," talking about someone else instead of confronting that person. "Aboutism," she says, "is a great sickness on any team. Talking to, not about, is how you make change happen."

So, when she hears someone comment on another individual's performance, she asks, "Have you given that person feedback?" and guides the person into thinking about solutions with questions like, "What can you do to help this team member?" and "As a team, what can you do to bring the person up to snuff?"

Getting and Giving Feedback

To help them handle situations like these, Zoby's team members have all had training in giving and getting feedback. The process they learned is a good guide for both coaches and team members.

For the person giving feedback, the rule is: Describe your feelings, the person's behavior, and the impact of that behavior on you personally. Put all this in the form of an I-statement. For example, say, "I'm frustrated when you don't come to work on time, because there are customers waiting and I don't get my other work done."

For the person getting the feedback, the rule is to say nothing about the feedback for twenty-four hours. Then decide what to do about it. After twenty-four hours, much of the defensiveness dissolves, but the significance of the feedback often remains.

Taking Disciplinary Action

All organizations have formal processes for taking documented disciplinary action against an employee when feedback and coaching fail. Such a process starts with counseling and moves through giving formal warning, putting the person on probation, and, finally, terminating the person's employment. When such worst-case scenarios occur, the most mature teams handle most of these steps themselves.

"In the past," says Bill Crockett of Texas Instruments, "the supervisor would go through formal disciplinary steps. Now, if I see a team has a problem, I ask, 'What are you going to do about it? Are you ready to take steps to administer discipline? Are you fed up enough?'"

The team may resist. One excuse is, "The former supervisor let it go on, and now you expect us to handle a problem he couldn't." Crockett tells the team members they are right, but they can't change the past; they can only be realistic today.

Crockett says that most of the teams in his shop handle responsibility for disciplining problem workers. Performance problems that get into the documentation and warning stage usually involve poor attendance or poor quality, he reports. Attendance records kept by the team coordinator provide documentation when the problem is in that area. If an employee surpasses allowable absences, the first step is for the coordinator and team members to discuss the problem with the employee and to find out whether there is a reasonable explanation, such as illness, or whether the person has simply been taking every Friday afternoon off. If the team decides that the employee is at fault, it issues an oral warning, giving the person thirty days to improve performance.

If the warning doesn't solve the problem, the team delivers written notice, "using good judgment first," Crockett says. In some teams, two or three people write up the guidance notice, which is then signed by either the whole team or a representative. Crockett approves the notice before it is delivered to the individual at fault. Or, he says, the team may give him the data and ask him to write the guidance notice. If the problem escalates and the team recommends probation, Crockett takes over from there.

He admits that every team isn't ready to handle the sensitivities and legalities of formal disciplinary action. If a team really can't handle the responsibility, he takes care of disciplinary action himself, he says. But he sees his primary function as tutoring the teams. "If they're going to confront an individual," he adds, "they know they have my backing."

He coaches them through the process, working closely with the coordinator. The policies, he says, are still in the old supervisor's handbook. Also, all personnel policies are on line, so everybody has access to them. "I explain that they have to follow the same policies the supervisors used to use."

But formal disciplinary action is a rarity in Crockett's or any other team-based environment. One of the best things about working with teams, managers report, is how seldom performance problems reach that stage.

14

Supporting Team Members' Career Development

When Joan Clarke of Motorola first told her team members that her job was to get rid of everybody, they reacted just as you might expect.

"They freaked out," Clarke recalls.

But, no, she wasn't announcing an impending downsizing or her desire to fire them all. She was promising them that she would help them look for opportunities to expand their skills, work in new areas, find out what they liked to do best, and grow in both their job satisfaction and their contributions to Motorola.

For some new workers, those are mind-blowing ideas. Diane Lewis is a supervisor now, but she says that when she started out on a line in Clarke's team, she had blinders on. Her only thought about work was to "come in, punch the start button, and let the board go." She did that very well. In fact, she was one of the fastest workers the team had, and in some organizations she'd have been encouraged to stay right there as long as she was willing, churning out those record production numbers.

Not in Motorola's Cellular Products Division. There, says Production Manager Michelle Thomas, the average production team job assignment lasts six to eighteen months, varying with business needs and the motivation of the people. It's the job of the supervisor—who is really a team coach, not a supervisor in the traditional sense—to interpret the business needs and to create an environment in which team members are motivated to see new career opportunities.

Says Thomas, "The supervisor widens people's horizons and lets them know there are other opportunities out there."

Clarke elaborates: "My job is to figure out what each worker wants to do and how that fits into our business." That's taking her role as mentor beyond what's required of her, since it's really the workers' responsibility to determine where they'd like to go in their careers. But she's sympathetic when workers can't always figure that out for themselves, admitting that "when I have to talk to my manager about my plans, I don't always know what to say."

"So," she adds, "it's up to me to give them some ideas, some exposure." She knows she's in a better position than most team members to know what the possibilities are, since she has contacts with her peers in other areas and they tell each other what positions are open.

A system for supporting team members' career development contains several components. It's important for team coaches to:

• *Prepare team members to excel in their current jobs.* Besides providing training and on-the-job coaching, this involves guiding them into making the most of the jobs they do now. The best team coaches help team members burst out of the narrow boxes that unnecessarily limit the way people see their positions.

At Bell Atlantic's Interexchange Carrier Service Center, service representatives set stretch goals, pushing the limits of what they can accomplish within their current jobs. This kind of goal setting can lead them to things that don't show up in their job descriptions but make their jobs more interesting and make them more valuable to the company.

To help the reps set goals, Team Developer Wilma Weed recommended that they look at what more they could do for the customer. But even one "incredibly customer-oriented" rep found it hard to come up with something new. "I've done so many things, I don't know what else I could do," she told Weed.

Weed encouraged her to think of a customer request that so far the team had done nothing about. The rep recalled meeting with a new customer to explain the company's bills and service. In frustration, the customer had exclaimed, "I don't know how to do business with Bell Atlantic. It's too complicated." Remembering that customer's frustration, the rep set a goal to create a brochure for new subscribers telling them how to do business with Bell Atlantic.

• *Prepare them to keep up with whatever the job may evolve into in the future.* Technology changes. Sometimes the organization's total direction changes; for example, Texas Instruments' Defense Systems and Electronics Group has had to move away from total dependency on the declining defense market. What people can count on is that even if they stay in the same job, it will look different five years from now. That's why Karen Page encourages her production workers to develop new skills, pointing out that the company may not need electronic assemblers forever.

• *Champion team members for temporary special assignments, project work, and cross-functional teams.* Look for opportunities for them to support marketing efforts, join cross-functional product development teams, take temporary assignments on other teams, or participate in other short-term projects that expand their skills, their exposure to other parts of the company, and their value to it. Some organizations even arrange for workers to spend time working in customers' or vendors' operations.

• *Encourage team members to seek out and move into new job assignments.* At Motorola, a group of materials expediters all came off production lines. And Diane Lewis lost her best machine operator to document control. Lewis sees that move as just one step in a developing career that could soon take the person to a new assignment, perhaps programming machines, she hypothesizes. "The issue is, how do we get the biggest utilization of what we put into people," Lewis says. Not by keeping a person in one job, she's convinced. "We'd better have a plan for each person," she asserts. It's important to provide each person with the opportunity to grow.

• *Encourage people to get the education they need to broaden their opportunities.* This may mean helping team members arrange flexible work schedules so that they can, if necessary, attend classes during the day. You may need to negotiate on someone's behalf not only with upper management but with the team itself, which makes work assignments.

• *Help team members become more valuable not only to your organization but to other employers as well.* Most people know that it's not realistic anymore to anticipate spending a lifetime with one organization. Yet, it's hard, while concentrating on the job at hand, to think about doing anything else. If you are serious about helping team members plan for the long term, you'll encourage them to build skills that will make them more attractive outside the organization as well as inside.

Tim Smith of Northern Telecom talks about this reality for employees there. "Included in our core values," he notes, "is the statement that 'People are our most important asset.' Yet we have layoffs from time to time." To uphold that value under those circumstances, Smith stresses that "we commit to making each employee the most employable person he or she can become." Teaching team members management skills is one way of doing that; giving them a broad base of work experience is another.

At Texas Instruments, Bill Crockett echoes the same sentiment. "Becoming multiskilled," he points out, "is a fundamental of self-directed work teams. It makes people more valuable to the company, and they would be more valuable to other companies too."

Part V

Facilitating Self-Management of Relationships

Connections can make or break an organization. Not political connections—that's not what this book is about. It's about the connections between people when work functions overlap or a product or a process gets handed off from one person or group to another. These are the sensitive places where success is as dependent upon good relationships as it is upon the quality of the product or service.

In a traditional, management-centered workplace, the supervisor keeps a close rein on what happens at these transfer points. Before making direct contact with other units, customers, vendors, upper management, or any other group, most employees are expected to follow their supervisor's injunction to "talk to me first." It is even the business of the supervisor to see to it that relationships between employees within the work unit are productive.

When teams become responsible for handling these relationships themselves, team coaches can help them by lubricating the connections that bind independent employees into a work team and that join the team to the outside world. In addition, because conflicts arise in even the smoothest operations, coaches need to be skilled mediators and to be able to help teams learn to manage conflict for themselves. The next three chapters address these functions of the team coach.

15

Building Teams Out of Independent Workers

Team building with self-directed work teams has two components. The first—the "self-directed" part—involves building and maintaining a team structure with defined responsibilities so that the group is directed and doesn't run off in all directions. The second component focuses on teamwork, or cooperation. Team members need to be willing to put the needs of the team ahead of their own, help each other, and modify the way they do their own job, if necessary, to improve team outcomes.

The first component deals with the formal relationships among team members, the second with informal relationships. This chapter examines the responsibilities of team coaches to help teams develop and maintain both.

Building Respect for the Team Structure

You don't tell a group of rugged individualists that from now on it will function as a self-directed work team and expect the members to cheer. Some of them are going to say, "Not me, folks, no way." They'll see team participation not as gaining power but as losing it, making them accountable to a whole group of people whereas, until now, they have had to answer to only one supervisor. If they are experienced workers who perform well, their supervisor has probably pretty much left them alone. Why would they want a whole team meddling in their work?

The team coach's first team-building task is to get people to participate.

Overcoming Resistance to Teaming

Many organizations, particularly if their workforce is unionized, don't force a team structure on their workers. When they implement SDWTs, they leave room in the operation for independents, or, as Ralph Galarneau, Titeflex's chief union steward, puts it, "teams of one." At best, teams of one are short-lived. As SDWTs gain momentum, peer pressure usually draws in the holdouts, especially when, as happened at Titeflex, the long-term employees—those other people look up to—buy in quickly.

In Krissan Zoby's group at Bell Atlantic, there are still some "traditionals" who have elected not to be on teams. Sometimes they move slowly, keeping a foot in both camps. She describes one person who has resisted a team's efforts to draw him in formally but who has contributed to that team during contests.

After trying to balance teams and independents for a time, however, some companies draw the line. According to Bill Crockett of Texas Instruments, "Over two to three years, we found out we couldn't have half the force on teams, half not. So we communicated that it's going to be everyone's job to work on a team."

And if workers still resisted? "Then this wasn't the place for them," Crockett concludes. "Some left of their own accord, some otherwise."

But they were the exceptions. For the most part in Crockett's unit, when "they saw we were serious and we gave them the tools, they came around. The strongest opponents can become the strongest proponents."

However, the change doesn't happen overnight. You should expect every team to go through the classic stages of team development, often dubbed Forming, Storming, Norming, and Performing.

In the *forming* stage, new team members are curious,

cautiously polite, but wary and generally self-protective. They want to know what teaming is about and what this particular team is about. They keep their antennae out to determine who is in charge: Who are the designated leaders? Who is emerging as a natural leader? They test the waters gingerly to discover where they fit in. They're willing to contribute but want to know what they will get in return.

When they begin to get comfortable in the team, members start to assert themselves, and that's when the *storming* phase begins. Differences of opinion erupt. Members test the limits of their power and sometimes overstep them — at least as perceived by others. The honeymoon is over, and the real working out of issues begins. It may not always feel good, but as they work through this phase, teams face up to underlying differences that would otherwise fester and undermine the group later.

Confronting differences leads to the *norming* stage, when teams develop both written and unwritten processes and standards of behavior that allow members to progress in a spirit of cooperation. Teams now have norms for effectively working together, or operating in the *performing* stage, when the business work of the team gets done.

Although performing is the fourth stage in a list of four, it would be naive to call it the final one, because any change in the team's equilibrium can cause the team to revisit earlier stages. The introduction of a new team member or the departure of an established one raises questions about what each person's role will be in the future, and the team will change shape and reform itself. An unanticipated change in business needs can reveal hitherto undetected differences that need to be reconciled in new norms before performance can return to its previous level.

As a team coach, there are actions you can take to support SDWTs as they go through these stages:

• Arrange for teams to get training in team development.

• Clarify for them what "empowerment" means in your organization. What are the boundaries? What is the team's jurisdiction?

• Listen to and validate the concerns and the feelings of team members. Never dismiss anyone's concerns, even if you think they are unwarranted. At the same time, encourage team members to take responsibility for resolving problems: "You are concerned that you'll lose control over scheduling your own work. Given the team's need to coordinate all the tasks, how do you think you can resolve that?"

• Encourage the team to listen to and validate each member's concerns and feelings in the same way. This is the way trust develops among members.

You may need to facilitate such discussions among team members. Zoby of Bell Atlantic describes a conversation about trust in one team in which a member described her ambivalence about sending a welcome-back card to a team member who had been out of work tending a sick mother. She'd decided not to send the card because she was afraid that the rest of the team would resent her doing so. By asking, "What could you have done about that?" Zoby got the employee to realize that she could have asked the others what they thought of the idea. "I'm bringing them around to being willing to speak up about their feelings," says Zoby. "We're still building trust."

• Assure the team that there will be no repercussions when things don't go as well as hoped. Take Zoby's advice and tell members, "Sometimes that's the way it is with teams." Then encourage them to move forward.

• Help them give each other feedback, using the techniques described in Chapter 13.

• Encourage them to solve problems by consensus.

Designating Team Roles

One of the first tasks facing SDWTs in the forming stage is the designation of team roles—naming people to assume the leadership role for each key process of the team. The roles are filled by volunteers for three months to a year, after which time team members rotate into new roles.

Each role carries with it a special relationship to the rest of the team, somewhat of a "first among equals." The team leader doesn't "boss" the rest of the team, for example; she prioritizes needs, develops meeting agendas, and facilitates team meetings, guiding the team to focus on its goals. The quality improvement leader doesn't tell people what to do to improve quality, but he does initiate activities aimed at making improvements happen.

The biggest challenge for any team role designee is to get the cooperation of the other people on the team. The team coach's role is to clear the path to cooperation by removing such obstacles as:

• *The rejection of the designee's authority by other team members ("Who are you to tell me what to do?").* Team members have just been released from the dominance of the supervisor. If they perceive that a team leader or quality improvement designee is trying to step into a similarly dominant role, they'll move quickly into the storming stage or, more subtly, quietly boycott their overzealous teammate's initiatives.

Solution: Convince people in team roles to get their teammates' input before they propose a new initiative. Wanda Vinson of Bell Atlantic explains this with a hypothetical incident: The team member in the quality improvement role announces a contest for team members and is confronted with frustrating resistance from teammates. A better approach, she points out, would be for the quality improvement person to solicit ideas from team members in advance and design the contest around their input. Their buy-in later would increase incrementally.

• *Members who have personal agendas that conflict with the ideas proposed by the person in the team role.* To push Vinson's example a little further, assume that one reason for team members' resistance to the quality contest is that they're striving to make more sales. For the contest they'd have to track their sales manually, since the system doesn't collect and output the information often enough to meet the goals of the contest. The team members think that manual tracking is a waste of time.

Solution: Keep them from chucking the baby out with the bathwater. Encourage them to develop options, working together to modify the initiative to meet everyone's needs. In the case of the quality contest, Vinson would ask the group, "How else can we capture the information?" Identifying the unsatisfactory component of the initiative and coming up with an alternative to it may draw in the resisters.

• *Team members who lack the confidence to tackle something new.* Returning to the example of the quality contest, some team members may privately be afraid they don't have the ability to deliver and don't want their failure made public. Rather than admit to their own insecurity, they may simply refuse to participate.

Solution: If you suspect that insecurity lies behind some team members' unwillingness to participate in team activities, start giving those people extra attention, Vinson recommends. If they take even a little step forward, show your appreciation. Make them feel important every day. Building people's self-confidence is a demanding task, Vinson admits. You do it with personal attention, such as recalling things they told you they are proud of and remembering to ask them about those things later. And you do it by offering them skill-building activities, such as workshops and pertinent audiotapes and following up with discussions of what they learned.

• *Teammates who don't have confidence in the person in the team role.* If the team as a whole lacks confidence in any one member, suggests Vinson, it's probably because the person lacks self-confidence and is unintentionally sending out that message.

Solution: Tackling this problem is a two-part task for the team coach, working first to help the individual and then to modify the team's attitude. If a work skills deficiency is holding the individual member back, arrange for him to get classroom or on-the-job training. If the person lacks smooth interpersonal skills, give her feedback and advice she can apply immediately, such as, "Look at people when you are talking to them," or "Write down what you want to tell people before you say it." Let her practice on you—and give plenty of positive feedback for each small improvement.

As the person gets stronger, advises Vinson, the team will need some team-building exercises in appreciating one another as a way to make team members aware of all the reasons they have to have confidence in each other. She suggests an activity: Put each team member's name on a brown paper bag, and post the bags on the wall for a week. Instruct team members to look for things to appreciate about one another: "I appreciated the information you shared with me when I had that problem call today." During the week, they are to write each appreciation on a note and drop it in the recipient's bag. At the end of the week, all team members are given their bags. They may read their notes to others if they wish, suggests Vinson, or keep them to themselves. That should be a personal choice.

Building Cooperation Among Team Members

In addition to raising team members' awareness of one another's value, the paper bag activity has another effect, Vinson adds. For a while, at least, it also makes people want to help one another. After all, no one wants an empty bag. So they open their eyes to each other's needs.

Building Awareness of Others

"Since so much of the work people here do is individual, they tend not to be aware of others," says Karen Page of Texas Instruments. "It's real important to force a dialogue, set aside time to talk about what's on your plate and mine."

Page urges team members to find out what their teammates need from them. "I ask a lot of questions," she says. The dialogue she describes goes something like this:

Page:	"Do you know your goal today?"
Team member:	"Sure, thirty boards."
Page:	"Do you know the goal of your next downstream person?"
Team member:	"No."
Page:	"Do you think it might be important for you to know?"
Team member:	"Yeah, I guess it is."

Page stresses that people have to know that what they do affects the entire shop both positively and negatively.

Diane Lewis of Motorola echoes the same thought: "Give them an understanding of how everything they do affects everybody. Start with something small," she advises, "for example, how defects on one line can shut down another line. When you see another person's frustration because you made a mistake, you're more concerned and you watch more."

Page recommends that team coaches look for and suggest ways that people can improve their work processes by working together. She gives some examples of how people are joining up in her circuit board operation:

"Each person has a computer screen with the instructions on line," she explains, "but we see two people side by side working off the same screen, doing two boards at one time. The result—they push each other and help each other with problems."

Part of the process of assembling the boards is stuffing in chips, and part is what the shop calls "make ready," checking the stuffed board for necessary hand work. In the past, Page says, the operators worked serially, stuffing lots of ten boards, and then handing off all ten to the make-ready person.

Now the assemblers work in pairs. One stuffs, and the

other takes each board out of the first one's hands to do make-ready. Through this interdependency, Page points out, they've discovered that they need their teammates. And they work faster.

When Page's team members discovered that two heads are better than one . . .

When, at Bell Atlantic, Krissan Zoby's team members created job aids with which to train one another on Saturdays . . .

When Motorola team members volunteered for other tasks — prepping, testing, helping other people — when their own operation ran out of parts and a line shut down . . .

. . . they had put aside their individualism. They were behaving like teams.

16

Mediating Conflict

It's inevitable. When you bring a group of people together and make them collectively responsible for running their business, they are going to have disagreements. There will be personality clashes, times when team members misinterpret each other's words, occasions when resentments and jealousies flair up, and situations in which people simply have strong differences of opinion about the best thing to do.

Managed productively, conflict can give birth to innovative new solutions and improved relationships based on better understanding of other team members' needs. Bill Crockett of Texas Instruments recalls, "We've had a couple of teams where shouting went on. People were yelling, 'And while we're at it, you're doing thus and such.' They got that behind them, cleared the air, and moved on."

Crockett thinks that those incidents were healthy. "When a team can get issues on the table, it allows them to get mistrust out of the way. These teams make the most progress," he asserts.

On the other hand, conflict that is swept under the rug can stifle creativity. Recall the situation described by Krissan Zoby of Bell Atlantic, in which one team member was so fearful of her teammates' disapproval that she decided against sending a simple greeting card to another employee who had been away from work. "They use avoidance as a method for handling potential conflict," Zoby notes.

Conflict that festers can poison relationships and slowly strangle the team's spirit. And conflict that is allowed to escalate can overwhelm the team and block its ability to accomplish anything.

The problem is not so much conflict itself as how teams deal with it. This chapter describes steps that team coaches can take to help teams convert conflict into better understanding and improved outcomes.

Key to all of them is one axiom: *Avoid giving advice.* Even if your advice is brilliant, in an emotion-laden situation it's unlikely to do anything but draw you into the conflict. Instead, ask questions that guide team members toward discovering their own solutions.

Conflict Between Two Employees

When one team member complains to you about another — "Mary Jo did this." "John didn't do that." "You gotta do something about Pat." — just remember that, as a team coach, you don't gotta do something about Pat. You do need to encourage the complainer to confront Pat about the situation in a constructive way.

Start by asking the obvious: "Have you talked to Pat about this?" You'll be amazed at how often the answer will be "no."

Then, encourage the complainer to look at the situation from the other person's point of view. Taking a tip from Karen Page of Texas Instruments, you might ask, "Can you give me three reasons why Pat might have done that?" It takes some of the edge off if the complainer realizes that Pat didn't necessarily behave out of spite or ignorance.

Help the complainer develop objective feedback to deliver to the other person. Using I-statements like the one recommended by Krissan Zoby of Bell Atlantic in Chapter 13 is a good approach. In an I-statement, the speaker takes ownership of his or her own feelings, describes the other person's behavior in specific, objective terms, and describes the impact of that behavior on the speaker. For example, "I'm disappointed that you developed the schedule without asking for my input because, as it stands, it does not allow me to complete my research project in time to meet my goal."

Such a statement avoids assigning motive ("Apparently you didn't care about my project!") or blame ("It's your fault I can't meet my goal."). It therefore decreases the likelihood that the other person will react defensively, escalating the conflict, rather than join in a problem-solving session.

Help the person who is about to confront the perceived wrongdoer by serving as an audience for a feedback rehearsal. You can even take the other person's part for an informal role-playing session. The more the person prepares for the confrontation, the more comfortable he or she will be and the more likely it will lead to a satisfactory solution for both.

Sometimes a conflict between two teammates becomes too hot for them to handle alone or the confronter is insecure about tackling the situation solo. Perhaps the teammates have already had a shouting match, and tempers are still high. Or perhaps you know neither of them is skilled yet at giving feedback and handling problem resolution.

In this case, offer to facilitate their meeting to resolve the issue. In Karen Page's operation, it's not unusual for someone to walk into her office and ask her to facilitate a discussion around a problem between the person and another worker. In the old days at Texas Instruments, Page would have taken on the problem and resolved it herself. Now, she says, "I've basically taken the approach that I'm available to help you work through it, but I'm not going to do your dirty work."

Wilma Weed of Bell Atlantic recalls an incident when teams were still new in her organization. "Two people really went at it," she remembers. "One criticized the other, telling her what she had done wrong, making her cry."

Because of the sensitivity of the situation, Weed began by talking privately to the person who had attacked the other so stridently, asking, "What do you think you could have done differently?"

"Maybe I could have suggested ways to do the work better instead of just saying what she did wrong," the employee admitted. So she made an appointment to discuss the issues with the person she had upset so badly. When they met, Weed was there to make sure that the meeting was safe for both of them.

When you facilitate a meeting between combatants, make sure they know the ground rule: Keep the discussion on observable behaviors. Weed clarifies this by contrasting two approaches to confronting a teammate in a situation ripe for conflict:

"One way to handle it would be to say, 'I wish you'd learn to get out of bed earlier because I have to do your work every morning.'"

She suggests a different dialogue to illustrate a better way:

Person 1: "I see you are coming in at 8:15 instead of 7:45. Have you changed your hours?"

Person 2: "No."

Person 1: "Are you aware that it puts a burden on the rest of us when you aren't here at 7:45? We get backed up. I have to do at least one extra order."

Call time-out when you hear a comment that falls into the category of the first approach: sarcastic, presumptuous, accusatory. Ask the person to reword the statement, describing the behavior strictly in terms of observable facts.

Move the focus to problem solving as quickly as possible. The key thing is to recognize that the problem to be solved is the negative impact of the behavior being addressed. Getting the "offender" to change behavior is one solution, but there may be others. In the example just given, the person coming late may be able to change officially to an 8:15 arrival by swapping with someone who has been coming in later. As in any problem-solving session, developing a list of possible solutions can contribute to a more satisfactory result.

The ideal resolution to a conflict is *win-win,* in which the combatants look beyond the symptoms and the rhetoric to the underlying concerns of each side and come up with a solution that addresses the real concerns of each. If you guide people through a problem-solving process that culminates in consensus, this is the outcome they'll achieve.

There are other approaches to resolving conflict, less ideal but often more expedient. These can be called:

- *No-win* — turning one's back and ignoring the problem. This "solution" is a cop-out when the issue is weighty but a relief if it's slight.
- *Lose-win* — capitulating and giving in to the other side; disastrous if the result is simmering resentment or loss of self-confidence but sometimes a plausible way to save energy for more important issues.
- *Win-lose* — fighting to the finish; a facilitator's nightmare but excusable in life-death situations.
- *Win a little/lose a little* — compromising — not bad if half a loaf is better than none, but useless when half a loaf means everyone goes hungry.

Here's how each of these might play out in the scenario suggested by Weed, with a team member coming in late each morning. Let's call the latecomer Chris and the sufferer Lee.

No-win: Lee and Chris never get around to discussing the issue.

Lose-win: Chris stops taking breakfast to the family next door whose mother is in the hospital and starts arriving on time regularly.

Win-lose: Chris goes over the team's head and gets permission from the vice president to arrive late while the neighbor is hospitalized.

Win a little/lose a little: Lee agrees to cover for Chris half the time and Chris talks another neighbor into providing breakfast on those days.

Obviously none of these solutions is as satisfactory as the win-win mentioned earlier: Chris formally switches hours with another teammate who's been arriving later.

As a conflict mediator, encourage the combatants to recognize their approach and name it. When they acknowledge their own behavior, they are more likely to shelve it and work for win-win or at least to save the other approaches for occasions when they'll do the least harm.

Conflict That Involves the Whole Team

When a team meeting disintegrates into a shouting match, take heart from the knowledge that out of disagreements can come a better way of doing things. Then apply all your conflict-mediation and problem-solving skills to achieve that outcome.

Here are steps a team coach can take to guide a conflict-ridden team from conflagration to cooperation.

1. *Help the team acknowledge its nonproductive behavior.* Ask, "What are we doing that's blocking resolution of the problem?" Encourage the team to avoid blaming others, making assumptions, and projecting motives. Look for responses like, "We're interrupting each other rather than listening. For example, I cut off Sally's comment about costs to make my point about outdated technology." Discourage remarks such as, "Sally's bringing up her old hobby horse about money again." When you hear comments like that, ask the speaker to rephrase them specifically and objectively.

2. *Help the team define the issue in terms of a shared need, rather than opposing points of view.* For example, "The problem is that we are missing deadlines" is a shared need. "The problem is that some of us want new computers and some of us want to save money by upgrading the old ones" is a statement of opposing points of view that will do little but solidify the difference.

3. *With the problem defined as a shared need, apply the problem-solving steps outlined in Chapter 9.* After defining the problem, encourage the team to identify causes, determine criteria, generate options, determine solution(s) through consensus, and develop implementation plans.

4. *During problem solving, keep the focus on issues, not personali-*

ties. The issue is that the team needs to find a way to meet its deadlines, not whether Sally is a cheapskate.

5. *When the team is determining criteria for a solution, encourage each side to propose and objectively explain its bottom-line requirements.* If you can get agreement here — for example, no overtime or a budget of $20,000 — the rest of the process will go much more smoothly.

6. *When they are generating options, keep reminding people of the brainstorming ground rule: no criticizing statements by other people.*

7. *Encourage everyone to listen to other points of view.* Ask people on one side of the argument to paraphrase statements by people on the other side.

8. *During the stage of identifying solutions, keep asking for points of agreement on which to base a win-win resolution.*

9. *Get everyone involved.* People who lean back and stay silent may be the ones to get everyone riled up again when the meeting is over. Get all the issues on the table and discussed.

10. *Don't stifle occasional outbursts of new anger.* Let them be heard, and then restate the issue objectively and encourage the team to move forward with problem solving.

Throughout the process, help team members express their feelings openly and honestly. Show them that they can disagree and still move on. Out of disagreement often comes a better solution.

17

Building Relationships Outside the Team

Motorola's team-based Cellular Products Division sends employees as far away as Japan to meet with customers. The travellers bring back in-depth understanding of the customer and the customer's special needs. They share that knowledge with their teammates.

What they carry with them when they travel is the mantle of Motorola. "Any time any employee meets a customer, to the customer that employee is the embodiment of Motorola," remarks Vice President Patty Barten. That person must represent the integrity, the quality, and the values on which Motorola stakes its reputation.

Making Contacts Outside the Company

There was a time when companies assumed that only managers were appropriate spokespersons for the organization. That assumption has gone by the wayside as evidence grows that front-line employees are often the best people to answer customers' detailed questions, to understand customers' needs, and to identify the most practical ways to build solutions into the development of the product or service.

The more teams assume control of the production or delivery of a product or service, the more they recognize the need for team members to build relationships with customers, to serve customers better, and to elicit better service from vendors.

Throughout this book have been several examples of such relationships:

- *Acquiring a new client.* A Titeflex employee/biker convinced Harley Davidson to use Titeflex flexible hose to replace rigid pipes on Harley motorcycles by demonstrating the superiority of his own retrofitted Harley.
- *Solving a vendor quality problem.* A manufacturing employee at Motorola figured out a solution to a supplier quality problem. First he called the designer; when he couldn't resolve the problem that way, he made an appointment with the president of the supplier company. He got the problem solved.
- *Hearing bad news from the horse's mouth.* When Titeflex workers visited a GE plant, GE employees told the visitors that the reason GE wasn't using much Titeflex hose was because Titeflex wasn't delivering on time. When the Titeflex employees took that news back to their peers, the situation changed fast.
- *Stepping into the marketing division's shoes.* At Bell Atlantic's Interexchange Carrier Service Center, service representatives have taken over responsibility for dealing directly with clients on billing questions. Until recently this kind of sensitive customer contact was the exclusive domain of marketing.
- *Shortening the chain of communication.* At GE's Plant III, when production team members ask Cell Leader Bill Harding when parts are expected from a vendor, he replies, "Here's the telephone number. Why don't you give them a call?"

How the Coach Can Help

There are a variety of actions a team coach can take to encourage teams to build relationships with vendors and customers and to smooth team members' paths as they strike out into unknown territory:

1. *Step aside if your participation clogs communication more than it contributes to it.* Like Harding, you can often just give team members the tools — such as a telephone number — and your blessing and let them make the contacts and develop their own relationships.

2. *Look for opportunities for teams to take over contacts formerly handled by people higher up on the organization chart.* Having the Bell Atlantic service reps take over billing from marketing expanded the reps' jobs, while freeing up marketing people to spend more time with prospective clients.

The people who give up the function may be dubious at first, wondering if your team members will handle it adequately. Show them how much time they'll save, and enlist their help to make the transition a smooth one. Then provide plenty of one-on-one support to the team members as they get used to performing their new tasks.

3. *Arrange for team members to visit clients to see firsthand how they use your product or service.* The Titeflex visit to GE was an ideal arrangement. Manufacturing workers from Titeflex met their counterparts at GE who were actually using Titeflex products in the engines they were making.

If a picture is worth a thousand words, a visit is worth a thousand thousand. It's the best way for the team to discover how it can improve its product or service to meet the client's needs.

4. *Open doors.* Got a team member with a good idea, like the Motorola employee who knew how to solve the vendor's quality problem? Get that person access to someone who can turn the idea into reality, even if it's the president of another company. If you don't have the right contacts yourself, then beat down doors in your own organization until you find someone who does.

5. *Go to bat for your team or a team member if someone else in your organization thinks your people are overstepping their bounds by communicating directly with people outside their own circle.* When the marketing people at Titeflex complained that the Harley rider was venturing into marketing territory by pitching Harley Davidson, his managers backed him up and were vindi-

cated when the Harley people liked the biker's suggestions better than marketing's.

If you are ever in doubt about the propriety of a relationship that crosses organizational lines, ask yourself just one thing: Does the team member have the knowledge to communicate effectively? In the end, it's expertise, not position, that makes a lasting impression.

Managing Relationships with Other Teams

It's not only relationships with people outside the organization that deserve nurturing. Communication between teams in your organization can get tricky, too. In an ideal world such relationships would always be supportive and cooperative; Krissan Zoby of Bell Atlantic tells of one artistic team member who creates fliers and graphs not just for her own teams but for other teams as well. Teams may be competitive—which isn't all bad if it results in higher production for all. Diane Lewis of Motorola gives an example: "If Joan's team builds two hundred transceivers, my team will want to do at least that."

But competition can breed less healthy attitudes than that which Lewis describes. At worst, relations between teams can break down into jealousies ("How come they got new equipment and we didn't?"), finger pointing ("It's the fault of the guy on the night shift"), and possessiveness ("No way we'll let them use our idea, our tools, our people!").

Facilitating communication between teams is a crucial part of the coach's job. To smooth out relationships among teams, team coaches can:

• *Focus team members' attention on organizationwide goals.* At Texas Instruments' McKinney Board Shop, says Karen Page, the focus is not just on the metrics of each team but on how they fit into the jigsaw puzzle of the McKinney Board Shop.

• *Advise them when their actions will affect another team.* Changing their use of shared resources, renegotiating with customers, altering the specs on a part or product—any of these can have a domino effect on another team. Encourage teams to talk to their counterparts before going ahead with any such action.

• *Encourage them to share resources and personnel.* At GE's Plant III, each shift has one cell leader for all four cells (teams). At the beginning of each shift, the cell leader meets with representatives of each cell in case they have to share workers or to resolve other issues that might develop across the four cells.

• *Encourage cross-training among teams.* The more skills team members have, the more valuable they are to the organization. When they have the skills to step temporarily into other jobs in other teams, the organization can respond flexibly to changes in customer demands by sharing personnel among the teams. In the process, people get to know each other better and appreciate each other more.

• *Facilitate joint decision-making meetings among representatives of all teams.* Chuck Stridde of Northern Telecom stresses that team coaches—called advisers in many Northern Telecom operations—must take a lead role in decision making that involves more than one team. "Teams make a lot of decisions about how work gets done," he notes, "but this gets tricky when they are trying to make a decision that affects other teams. Advisers facilitate discussion among the teams, using consensus methodology."

Part VI

Success and Its Aftermath

In the final analysis, the success of a team can be measured by its contribution to the financial health of the organization. But how do organizations measure the success of team coaches? Is it fair to assume that when teams are profitable, the coach is responsible? Or that when teams fall short of their goals, the coach is to blame? Because the impact of the team coach is so indirect in comparison to that of a traditional supervisor, the question of what it is appropriate to hold a coach accountable for is much less clear.

This part of the book examines this question from two points of view: that of the organization and that of the coaches themselves. It looks at the standards team-based organizations use to evaluate team coaches' performance and at how coaches measure themselves.

Finally, the book looks into the future with the question, Can self-directed work teams get so competent that they don't need coaches anymore? Is there such a thing as an empty-nest syndrome for coaches? If so, what's next for them? The final chapter describes how some team coaches expect to apply their new skills a few years from now.

18

Measuring Success

Ask team coaches how their organizations measure their performance and you get some surprising answers. Surprising, not because the measurements sound as new and revolutionary as the job, but because for the most part they are so traditional. Some typical answers:

- "Production control, quality, the team's performance."
- "Making sure teams get the work done."
- "Quality, production, costs, environment, health and safety, integrity."
- "50 percent people development, 50 percent accountable for results."
- "Maintaining the line of balance; if the schedule calls for eight widgets a day for eight days, maintaining that."
- "Meeting customers' needs. Delivering the product on time at the lowest cost and highest quality."
- "Meeting financial goals, such as for shipments and scrap."
- "Customers being serviced in a timely manner with a quality product."

The bottom line has not changed. Team coaches are judged on results, just as supervisors always have been. As Karen Page of Texas Instruments explains, "It's still all about execution. Even where I've turned responsibilities over to the team, I'm responsible for getting them to execute them."

Results Plus Team Development

As important as results are, great numbers aren't all the team-based organization looks for when it measures the performance of a team coach. Chuck Stridde of Northern Telecom explains the added dimension: "The coach or adviser is accountable not so much for the performance of work as for where the team is in its development." Of course, in many respects, team development is measured by bottom-line results. The key is that, at each stage in its development, it accomplishes those results with less and less management involvement.

As Tom Howes of Texas Instruments says, "You are successful when your teams are capable of on-time delivery, reduction of cycle time, and reduction of staff, and you can withdraw and become a resource."

He illustrates with an example: "Are you really helping them figure out how to reduce cycle time? Your task is to be successful by helping people understand how to improve it, not to improve it yourself."

Accountability Without Authority

It sounds like an uncomfortable paradox: being held accountable for results despite not being able to act directly to make those results happen. All the standard management literature warns against making someone accountable for an outcome without giving the person the authority to make it happen.

Team coaches who can't live with the paradox often self-select out of the role. Those that embrace it find that trust is as powerful as authority for getting work done by others.

Wilma Weed of Bell Atlantic gives an example. "I'm accountable," she states, "for making sure 'dates due' are not missed. My boss is going to come to me if they are. But the team is responsible for the daily distribution of work and making sure it gets done. I'm trusting them to determine how to accomplish our top priority, meeting customers' dates due."

Why is she so confident? "I tell them if they are ever going to miss a date due to tell me; I need to know," she explains. "What actually happens is they find ways to accomplish what needs to be done. They have not let me down. Usually they find their own resources. But if they run into a brick wall, they come and say, 'I've done this, this, and this. Will you help?' That's when I get involved."

At GE, Cell Leader Bill Harding has a quick answer when he's asked what he's held accountable for. "Everything," he replies. That includes quality, production, cost, and all the other standard metrics of a manufacturing operation. How does he feel about accountability without traditional authority? It doesn't seem to have clipped his wings. "I run this place," he says with a chuckle, insisting he'd rather "run" it the new way by getting five or six individuals in each cell to perform as a self-directed team, rather than by telling everyone what to do.

Who Judges the Coach?

While the measurements on which team coaches are judged are largely traditional ones, the people doing the judging often are not traditional at all. Instead, 360-degree appraisal is increasingly becoming the norm.

Smith of Northern Telecom reports that one third of the input into his performance evaluation comes from team members, one third comes from peers, and one third comes from his manager. Team members and manager use four-point rating scales; peers use a system in which they vote for half of their colleagues in each of ten categories. This system is comparable to the team members' peer appraisals described in Chapter 11. Samples of Northern Telecom forms used by team members and peers are presented in Figure 18–1.

Of the several offices reporting to Krissan Zoby's boss,

Figure 18-1. Sample performance evaluation forms for coaches.

The EVALUATE-YOUR-MANAGER Form

Employee Evaluation of _____
(manager's name)

The purpose of this form is to improve employee satisfaction and give managers specific feedback that will help them improve their people management skills. The ratings you give your managers on this anonymous evaluation will count 30% towards their final official performance rating. To preserve your anonymity, you may type the comments page or have a relative or friend write out your comments. Please be as fair, accurate, and specific as you would like your manager to be on your evaluation. Please return this evaluation to the designated box within three business days.

Please check one box to the right of each numbered statement that best describes your manager's performance.

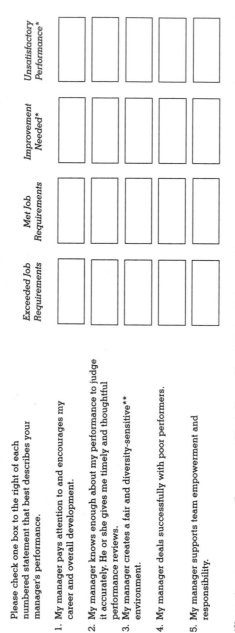

	Exceeded Job Requirements	Met Job Requirements	Improvement Needed*	Unsatisfactory Performance*
1. My manager pays attention to and encourages my career and overall development.	☐	☐	☐	☐
2. My manager knows enough about my performance to judge it accurately. He or she gives me timely and thoughtful performance reviews.	☐	☐	☐	☐
3. My manager creates a fair and diversity-sensitive** environment.	☐	☐	☐	☐
4. My manager deals successfully with poor performers.	☐	☐	☐	☐
5. My manager supports team empowerment and responsibility.	☐	☐	☐	☐

*If you give your manager an "Improvement Needed" or an "Unsatisfactory Performance" in any category, you must give an explanation on the back page in order for your rating to count.
**i.e., sensitive to employee diversity in terms of race, color, religion, gender, age, marital status, sexual orientation, national origin, or disability.

(name)	Commitment to People Development	Quality of Dept's Performance	Timeliness of Response to Request	Customer Focus Internal	Customer Focus External	Ease of Dealing With	Role Model	Commitment to Excellence	Contribution to NRDC's Success	Met MFA Objectives
(name)	—	—	—	—	—	—	—	—	—	—
(name)	—	—	—	—	—	—	—	—	—	—
(name)	—	—	—	—	—	—	—	—	—	—
(name)	—	—	—	—	—	—	—	—	—	—
(name)	—	—	—	—	—	—	—	—	—	—
(name)	—	—	—	—	—	—	—	—	—	—
(name)	—	—	—	—	—	—	—	—	—	—
(name)	—	—	—	—	—	—	—	—	—	—
(name)	—	—	—	—	—	—	—	—	—	—
(name)	—	—	—	—	—	—	—	—	—	—
(name)	—	—	—	—	—	—	—	—	—	—
(name)	—	—	—	—	—	—	—	—	—	—

Vote for 6

Source: Tim Smith, business unit manager, Northern Telecom. Used with permission.

hers is the only one with self-directed work teams. Performance appraisals are therefore still geared to the way things were. Nevertheless, Zoby and her peers ask for input into their appraisals from team members, "my clients, if you will."

Crockett of Texas Instruments distributes performance appraisal forms to teams and to his peers. Then he sits down with his peers, not his boss, for an appraisal meeting.

The change to peer appraisals doesn't come easy. When you and your colleagues are all in a new role, giving objective feedback can be awkward. "We have anonymous quarterly peer appraisals," reports Page, also of Texas Instruments. "The first time everyone said only good things. Then we forced ourselves to say one good and one bad."

Despite its difficulty, 360-degree appraisal for team coaches has benefits for the organization, the coach, and the teams:

* *It provides feedback from the people closest to the action.* Management can see the results achieved by the team, but it can't always see the processes involved in achieving them as clearly as team members and peers can. Team members feel the impact of every action the team coach takes to guide the team to self-management. And peers experience the result of actions that involve other parts of the organization.

* *It offers the benefit of providing many points of view.* A traditional appraisal is done from a single point of view. When that viewpoint is combined with input from team members and peers, the result is much richer and three-dimensional.

* *It offers additional credibility for the team system.* "They don't work for me anymore; I work for them," is a common remark from team coaches trying to explain their new relationship with team members. Giving team members input into the coach's appraisal supports that philosophy.

* *It provides a role model for the team.* If it's difficult for coaches to perform peer reviews, it's no easier for teams. As they mature, however, performing such reviews is one of the things that's expected of them. It's helpful to them to know that teams of coaches are struggling with and resolv-

ing the same issues that are facing the teams. Coaches who have been through the process themselves are also better prepared to support teams of workers when they assume responsibility for evaluating their teammates.

Self-Assessment

The organization measures the coach on numbers; the team measures the coach on helpfulness along its route to self-management; peers measure the coach as a team player in the management team. Team coaches have their own standards for success. When they appraise their own performance, they judge themselves on two criteria:

1. *How much team members grow on the job.* "I want to help other people the way my supervisors helped me," states Diane Lewis of Motorola. A product of the team system herself, she, like many of her peers, measures her success by the people she motivates to move on to new opportunities.

2. *How well they master the challenge of organizational change.* Switching to SDWTs is one of the great adventures in organizational transformation. It is nothing short of an upheaval in business as we've known it, an upending of the status quo. For team coaches, success resides in watching the revolution lead to a more productive workplace and knowing they've contributed to the change.

19

Looking Ahead

If the goal of a team coach is to transfer management skills and responsibilities to the team, what happens to the job when the team can do it all? Does success make the coach obselete?

Some say "yes."

"I shouldn't be here," asserts Bill Harding of GE. "My number one goal is to work myself out of a job."

Krissan Zoby of Bell Atlantic anticipates a time when her organization will need fewer coaches than it has now. "Today, supporting four teams is next to impossible, but someday it will be possible," she projects. "We're management top-heavy," she admits. "We'll be eliminating management people. It's most important to provide team members skills and development so they can take over what I do."

The operation that Bill Crockett manages for Texas Instruments has already eliminated its facilitators, who were former supervisors. "We matured beyond them," he says. What coaching still needs to be done he handles, aided by support people in areas such as training, quality, and safety.

This doesn't mean that the axe fell and the supervisor/facilitators were all left out on the street. Crockett admits that there were some casualties, people who found it too hard to adapt to the new realities, but most of the former supervisors transitioned into resource areas that support production. "This is not make-work," Crockett affirms. "It is really something needed. We don't have enough of them now."

The Case for Expanding the Coach's Role

In other team-based operations, the expectation is that the role of team coach will evolve, rather than disappear.

Vice President Patty Barten of Motorola says that she is often asked, "What is there left for management to do?" But building and maintaining an operation of self-directed work teams offers more, not less, opportunity for managers, including supervisors, she insists. As teams have taken on day-to-day management, supervisory responsibilities haven't diminished, Barten says. Rather, they have shifted "from what gets built today to where to take the business for the rest of the year."

Indeed, if transferring management tasks were the coaches' sole responsibility, the job should get easier as teams get more competent. But, although they are well past the teaming start-up stage, Supervisors Joan Clarke and Diane Lewis of Motorola both insist that it was easier, although less rewarding, to supervise the old way. Their focus now is on people development, and they don't expect the need for that to go away.

Karen Page of Texas Instruments also sees the team coach role as an evolving and expanding one. "Rather than move from one facilitator for thirty people to one for a hundred people, you pick up additional responsibilities in the support area, such as cost reduction. These round out who you are. I don't see my role going away. I see facilitator becoming a subset of a person's role.

"For example, I have to do three cost reviews and a budget by the end of today."

Team coaches should expect that a few years from now they'll be doing some very different things, whether they are in new jobs or have new job descriptions. Even now, as pioneers in an experiment that has just begun to rock the foundations of the business world, most coaches know that their most valuable attribute is flexibility, a willingness to change. That quality, along with the drive to acquire knowledge and experience in a range of disciplines, will be even more important in the future.

That's why Patty Barten at Motorola puts a heavy emphasis on helping people acquire a wide range of life and professional experiences. These might include, for a production supervisor, a tour of duty in China and lateral moves into other operations, such as planning and scheduling. "We believe in the value of lateral movement," she explains, "to give people the breadth of experience that facilitates eventual upward progression. We even encourage bizarre rotations. We've had people with doctorates in prestigious disciplines from M.I.T. ask to become production supervisors."

Of course, a team coach—or anyone else, for that matter—who sits back and waits for his employer to send him to China to round out his developmental experiences is going to have a long wait. A more likely winner in the career sweepstakes is the person who manages her own career, seeks out new possibilities, volunteers for new responsibilities, and places herself in the forefront of change.

As production control supervisor for GE's Plant III, Joe Reece is already in a position that supports all the teams in the plant. He moved to his current assignment from the drastically flattening management track because, as he says, "I've managed my growth. I like to get involved in something, do it until it gets routine, then hop onto the next bus. If you have a history showing you can be in the forefront of change, that opens doors."

One characteristic of Reece's history is that he's never been afraid to make a move that looked like a step backward to other people if he knew it would broaden his experience. He did that in 1985 when GE converted Plant III into its automated Factory of the Future. From being a unit manager with several foremen reporting to him in the previous organization, Reece took the position of cell leader in the automated plant. It was a job that evolved according to unique needs, he recalls. Although some people thought he'd taken a demotion, for Reece the experience led to a promotion to operations manager, just one step down from plant manager, which was a nice spot to be in until the plant closed down in 1992 to reinvent itself into its present team-based organization.

When that big change came in 1992, all jobs in the plant were open to bids, and people posted for them, whether they had worked in the plant all their working lives or had never set foot in Plant III. Again, Reece was ready for change, undaunted by a new structure that eliminated the management ladder. He describes his job as involving lots of communication, scheduling, raw materials procurement, inventory management, planning, and "lots of things that used to be done by three or four different functions."

Where to Next?

What Reece's work history illustrates is that there are opportunities to pursue new challenges even in dramatically flattened organizations. Wilma Weed of Bell sees potential opportunities all around, and she's preparing herself for a variety of possibilities. "I've been writing some marketing materials that have to be consistent throughout Bell Atlantic," she relates. "And I see us taking over more training as Bell Atlantic downsizes. Another thing—as technology gets crazier and crazier, just keeping track could be a job for somebody."

She sums up optimistically, "There are so many possibilities of jobs to go to within the company because of this experience."

But it's also true that those possibilities are much less likely than they were a decade ago to be on higher rungs of the corporate ladder.

For some team coaches, dimished upward mobility is a loss they mourn but know they have to live with. Karen Page's boss was not replaced when he was promoted into a new position recently. "They wanted to flatten the organization," she says. On the one hand, she adds, "we feel good the organization thinks we're capable of working without him. At the same time, we're disappointed they didn't pick one of us to fill the job."

She wonders what skills the organization looks for when it does promote someone. Her former boss, she says, has authority and commands attention. But these qualities, she recognizes, are completely different from the consensus-building skills needed by facilitators. She describes her own strengths as fostering consensus, getting along with others, and adapting to the changing environment. "But does this make me promotable?" she wonders. "Or is the old-line manager more suitable for promotion?"

For other team coaches, reduced opportunities for promotion are of little concern. Dave Litwin of Titeflex says, "I don't think I want to be a vice president. I'm best suited for being on the floor." What he wants, he adds, is to be rewarded for doing what he does best with a share in the profits of the company.

At Northern Telecom, Tim Smith is pragmatic. "Regarding career advancement," he says, "the old-style management careers are going. You have to change if you want to continue a career, let alone advance."

What many of these pioneering team coaches look forward to in the future is a chance to take teaming beyond their present workplaces. Says Smith, "With what I've learned about teams, I think I could be an asset to any company with teams or wanting to implement them."

Weed looks forward to advancing teams throughout Bell Atlantic. "A couple of years down the road, we may have fewer team developers here, but we're just at the beginning of self-directed work teams in the company," she says. "Every department is looking at them now. If I had to leave this job, I could go someplace else with the skills I've learned."

Her colleague Wanda Vinson feels the same way. "I hope to become an expert on implementing self-direction. That's the way organizations are going. Even if this job were to close, I see potential for me to support this new workstyle somewhere. That's the career I'm trying to orchestrate for myself."

Although it's true that, as teams mature, many companies do reduce the number of coaches supporting them, there is little fear among team coaches that theirs is a temporary, limited job. Instead, they view their work as a growth opportunity, a chance to gain skills that they can apply in a broader business arena. For them, the future is just beginning.

References

Doyle, M., and D. Straus. *How to Make Meetings Work.* New York: Jove Books, 1976.

Fisher, K. *Leading Self-Directed Work Teams.* New York: McGraw-Hill, 1993.

Fogg, C. D. *Team-Based Strategic Planning: A Complete Guide to Structuring, Facilitating, and Implementing the Process.* New York: AMACOM, 1994.

Harrington-Mackin, D. *The Team Building Tool Kit.* New York: AMACOM, 1994.

Kepner, C. *Team Decision Making: A Practical Guide to Making It Work.* Eden Prairie, Minn.: Wilson Learning, 1992.

Orsburn, J., L. Moran, E. Musselwhite, and J. Zenger. *Self-Directed Work Teams: The New American Challenge.* Homewood, Ill.: Business One Irwin, 1990.

Quick, T. *Successful Team Building.* New York: AMACOM, 1992.

Wellins, R., W. Byham, and G. Dixon. *Inside Teams: How 20 World-Class Organizations Are Winning Through Teamwork.* San Francisco: Jossey-Bass, 1994.

Wynn, R., and C. Guditus. *Team Management: Leadership by Consensus.* Columbus, Ohio: Merrill, 1984.

Zenger, J., E. Musslewhite, K. Hurson, and C. Perrin. *Leading Teams: Mastering the New Role.* Homewood, Ill.: Business One Irwin, 1994.

Index